Table of Contents

Dedicated to the "Three Girls"

Jackie, Johanna & Christina
—excellent field companions!

Orchids
of
New England
&
New York

Orchids
of
New England
&
New York

By Tom Nelson & Eric Lamont

Kollath+Stensaas
PUBLISHING

Kollath+Stensaas Publishing
394 Lake Avenue South, Suite 406
Duluth, MN 55802
Office: 218.727.1731
Orders: 800.678.7006
info@kollathstensaas.com
www.kollathstensaas.com

ORCHIDS *of* NEW ENGLAND & NEW YORK

Printed in South Korea by Doosan
10 9 8 7 6 5 4 3 2 1   First Edition

Editorial Director: Mark Sparky Stensaas
Graphic Designer: Rick Kollath

Illustrations by Rick Kollath, Kollath Graphic Design
www.kollathdesign.com

Cover photos by Tom Nelson: Clockwise from top: Showy Lady's-slipper (*Cypripedium reginae*), Calypso (*Calypso bulbosa* var. *americana*), Yellow Fringed Orchid (*Platanthera ciliaris*), Tuberous Grass-Pink (*Calopogon tuberosus* var. *tuberosus*).

ISBN-13: 978-1-936571-04-8

Acknowledgements

Tom thanks his family, starting with his parents Tom and Shirley Nelson, who inspired and supported his love of nature from an early age; his wife Jackie and daughters Johanna and Christina who are his mostly uncomplaining "support crew" and have accompanied him to some of the most spectacular orchid sites of North America.

Eric expresses sincere appreciation to his wife Mary Laura, who has shared 30+ years of wonderful botanizing and bird watching throughout eastern North America; his grandmother and parents, who nurtured his love for nature at an early age; and children Jessica and Caleb for family adventures to the Great Smoky Mountains, Mount Washington, Florida, and elsewhere.

We have crossed paths with many individuals who have shared our passion for native orchids and we are grateful for their unselfish sharing of information, localities, photographs, and especially for sharing incredible experiences in the field. Special thanks go to Charles "Chuck" Sheviak for patiently answering many questions on difficult taxa, identifying questionable species from photographs, and sharing localities. Eleanor "Sam" Saulys guided us to great orchid sites, shared vast knowledge and photographs, and reviewed draft species descriptions and distribution maps. Scott Shriver generously lent us his private orchid capsule collection to supplement ours for images in this book, provided hand-drawn maps and field notes to obscure orchid localities, and provided a custom built black velvet background for photographing. Paul Martin Brown has been our orchid friend for many years; he shared valuable locality data on orchid "hot spots" throughout New England, and first introduced Tom to Eric.

We thank our photographer friends Jim Fowler, Charles Ufford, Sylvain Beausejour, Scott Shriver, Eleanor "Sam" Saulys and Lorne Heshka for contributing great images to round out this book. Thanks also to Kim & Cindy Risen for their great images. We acknowledge noted flower photographer Ron Parsons who introduced Tom to the wonders of ring flash photography.

Expeditions into the field searching for native orchids have been the most gratifying aspect of preparing this book. We are sincerely grateful to many friends for sharing these field experiences with us in remote habitats where orchids hide and reside. The de facto leaders of the central New York "orchid gang" include Charles Ufford and Matthew Young, along with Kenneth Hull, and Bard Prentiss. Years ago, Richard Mitchell organized several field trips to orchid "hot spots" throughout New York. For assistance in the field throughout southeastern New York and northern New Jersey we thank Karl Anderson, Jim Ash, David Austin, Tom Halliwell, Linda Kelly, Robert McGrath, Janet Novak, Richard Stalter, Mark Szutarski, David Taft, and John Turner. In addition to those previously acknowledged, George Newman and Dennis Magee guided us to various orchid localities in New Hampshire. And we would be remiss in not remembering the contributions of the late Joe Beitel and the late Steven Clemants.

We acknowledge with gratitude the following people who helped us find many of the species that were photographed for this book in localities throughout North America: Steve Baker, Cathy Bloome, Adam Cousins, Frank Di Stefano, Robert Freeman, Kathleen Garness, Ron Hanko, Lorne Heshka, Mark Larocque, Warren Mazurski, Al Menk, Richard Reeves, Hans Roemer, and Ben Rostron.

We thank Jackie Kallunki for discussions on *Goodyera* and, along with Lisa Fruscella, assistance in the herbarium at The New York Botanical Garden; Gustavo Romero for assistance in the herbarium at Harvard University Herbaria; and Diana Hurlbut for assistance in researching journal citations for New York orchids. We also thank Kerry Barringer, Steven Glenn, David Werier, and Stephen Young for sharing orchid data stored at their respective institutions.

Thanks to our great editor, Sparky Stensaas, for his keen eye, editorial acumen, and dedication to the natural world. Thanks also to Rick Kollath for his superb illustrations.

—Tom Nelson and Eric Lamont.
May 15, 2012

The publishers would like to thank Tom Nelson and Eric Lamont for their enthusiasm and dedication to the study of orchids and sharing it with the world. Their passion comes through in their writing and in Tom's stunning photos. Thanks guys!

The publishers
May 11, 2012

Preface

Why are some people obsessed with orchids? It's not a new phenomenon. For more than 350 years, accounts have been published about botanists attacked by "savages," disappearing in wild places, dying of diseases, dying of spear wounds and gunshot wounds, enduring unimaginable hardships, all in pursuit of orchids. These individuals think nothing of traveling hundreds or thousands of miles just to observe a single orchid. Back in the days of Morris & Eames, authors of *Our Wild Orchids* (1929), those many miles were traversed over many more days than now. The naturalist John Muir wrote that he "shed tears of pure joy" over the beauty of Calypso, after meeting it for the first time in the depths of a lonely swamp. It must be a shared passion that binds these individuals together.

The two of us share this passion for wild orchids. And don't be fooled, we also have had life-threatening experiences while sleuthing for orchids—like almost getting stuck in hip-deep quicksand. Our first outing together was a November trip to the North Fork of eastern Long Island, New York, in search of *Tipularia* leaves. The trip was a success and that following April we met in the Great Smoky Mountains for brilliant displays of *Galearis spectabilis* and *Cypripedium parviflorum* var. *pubescens.*

Some of our most memorable orchid encounters include searching for and finding flowering *Triphora* in a hemlock-beech forest south of Mount Washington, New Hampshire, and scattered colonies of *Cypripedium arietinum* on a large chunk of limestone in Lake Chaplain known as Valcour Island. It was a real treat to visit a fen festooned with *Cypripedium reginae*, during a one-day visit to central New York State. The experience of finding 100 densely clustered individuals of Calypso in full flower has been one of life's highlights. We felt privileged to be shown blooming specimens of *Isotria medeoloides*—one of the rarest orchids in North America—in Maine.

Even though we have observed in the field all orchids covered in this book, there is always so much more to learn about these elusive denizens of secret places, and the mighty winds of change are once again blowing in the academic world of orchids. Should *Coeloglossum* be included in *Dactylorhiza*, and *Listera* in *Neottia*? Should *Gymnadeniopsis* be separated from *Platanthera*?

We hope you find this guide to be a useful companion on your orchid forays into the wonderful and varied wild areas of New England and New York. Happy hunting!

—Tom Nelson & Eric Lamont

What is an Orchid?

With over 30,000 known species, orchids are one of the largest families of flowering plants on earth. With the exception of Antarctica, wild orchids occur throughout the world, in virtually all terrestrial environments hospitable to life, even within the Arctic Circle. There is tremendous variety in the orchid family: one Central American species has flowers no larger than the head of a pin, while at the other extreme a species in New Guinea has stems 15 feet in length! Orchid flowers can be irresistibly showy—like *Cattleya*, a favorite of the florist trade—or small, dull colored and nondescript, eliciting a response of "that's it?" when first seen. And don't forget that vanilla extract comes from an orchid—appropriately, the Vanilla Orchid.

The unsurpassed beauty and exotic allure of many orchid species has fascinated mankind for centuries. In Victorian England collecting and discovering reached such a fever pitch that those afflicted with this flower madness were said to have "orchidelirium." Wealthy orchid fanatics sent explorers and collectors to almost every part of the world in search of new species of orchids. The thrill of the hunt continues to the present day and with over 200 species of orchids native to the United States and 65 species and varieties in New England and New York, the modern-day orchidophile will never be bored.

All living organisms are classified by kingdom, phylum, class, order, family, genus and species, based on biological and anatomical similarities. Lesser taxonomic ranks like subspecies, variety and forma are used to recognize variation within a species. Varieties and subspecies generally have a defined range and produce offspring that resemble the parent; forma are typically random variations occurring within a population.

The orchid family (Orchidaceae) is a member of the class of plants called the angiosperms (Angiospermae), the flowering plants. There are two subclasses within the angiosperms: the monocots (Monocotyledonae) and the dicots (Dicotyledonae). Cotyledons are the embryonic seed leaves

---

Characteristics of Orchids:
- Stamens and pistils (male and female parts) fused together into a single structure unique to orchids known as a column
- Modified stigma known as rostellum serves to transfer pollinia to pollinators, frequently through amazing methods
- Three petals and three petal-like sepals usually with one highly modified petal called the labellum or lip
- Flower stems twist as they develop via process called resupination
- Pollen usually in masses known as pollinia
- Seeds are tiny, numerous and lack endosperm (food supply)

---

contained within a seed—monocots have one; dicots have two. Orchids, along with grasses, palms and lilies, are considered monocots, even though their tiny seeds contain no cotyledon. They are classified in the order Asparagales, which also includes some of our choicest flowering plants such as day lilies, daffodils, irises, crocuses and amaryllis, as well onions, leeks, garlic and of course, asparagus.

Two of the features shared by most monocots are parallel leaf venation and flower parts in cycles of three. Small Purple Fringed Orchid (see *Parts of an Orchid* illustration on page 5) perfectly illustrates these floral traits, with its six flower parts consisting of three sepals and three petals, while the foliage of the Pink Lady's-slipper clearly demonstrates the conspicuous parallel venation of the typical monocot leaf. One of the petals of the orchid flower is modified into a lip or labellum—a key characteristic of the family—and acts as a landing pad that directs the pollinator toward the nectary. This modified lip has evolved to attract specific insect pollinators and its oftentimes fantastically altered shape can be exotically beautiful, like Arethusa, or just plain bizarre, like Hooker's Orchid. In most orchids the stem twists around as the flower opens, displaying the lip in the lower or resupinate position. But in some orchids, such as the Tuberous Grass Pink, there is only a slight twist and the lip is held uppermost. This is known as a non-resupinate flower.

What IS NOT an Orchid...Beware the Imposters!

There are a few wildflowers you may encounter that upon first glance could be mistaken for an orchid. Beware the imposters! Fringed Polygala (*Polygala paucifolia*) is an early blooming pink-blossomed beauty that you will find in the company of pines. Cousins Indian Pipe (*Monotropa uniflora*) and Pinesap (*Monotropa hypopithys*) are both saprophytes that lack green chlorophyll as in some orchids (*Corallorhiza*/Coralroot species). A cursory examination will quickly separate these imposters from true orchids.

Pinesap
(*Monotropa hypopithys*)

Fringed Polygala
(*Polygala paucifolia*)

Indian Pipe
(*Monotropa uniflora*)

Orchid Biology 101

In orchids, the male stamen and female pistil are united into the column, a structure unique to the orchid family. Orchids produce large masses of pollen—known as pollinia—that are attached to either side of the column; fertilization is completed when the pollinator brushes into the column and deposits attached pollen on its way to the nectary. The various shapes and positions of the lip, column and pollinium are evidence of a high degree of specialization in orchids and these structures have evolved in specific ways to attract and direct pollinators.

The subject of orchid pollination so intrigued Charles Darwin that he devoted years of study to the topic and published a landmark book, *The Various Contrivances by Which Orchids Are Fertilized by Insects*. Bees, butterflies, moths, wasps, flies, and hummingbirds are some of the

Charles Darwin.

known pollinators of orchids. Many orchids, such as Eastern Prairie Fringed Orchid, emit a fragrance at a certain time of day or night to attract a specific pollinator. Some orchid species, such as Autumn Coralroot, have closed (cleistogamous) self-fertilizing flowers that never open.

Unlike most flowering plants that have an ovary that ripens at the center of the flower, the orchid ovary is situated beneath the flower and resembles a swollen stem. A typical seed pod can hold hundreds of thousands and even millions of minute seed—the smallest of any flowering plant—that lack any stored food source, or endosperm.

In orchids, one flower petal (the lip or labellum) is highly modified in shape, color and structure; usually to aid in insect pollination.

In order to survive after germination, the orchid seed must establish a mycorrhizal relationship with a symbiotic fungus to provide the necessary nutrients for seedling development. These associations are not highly specific, and orchids are able to form relationships with a variety of parasitic and saprophytic soil fungi.

The fungus consists of a vegetative part known as the mycelium, made up of hundreds of tiny threadlike cells called hyphae that form an extensive network throughout a large area of soil and essentially act as an extensive root system for the developing orchid seedling. When the hyphae penetrate the orchid embryo they are utilized as a food source and furnish the needed nutrients for seedling development. It takes several years before

Parts of an Orchid

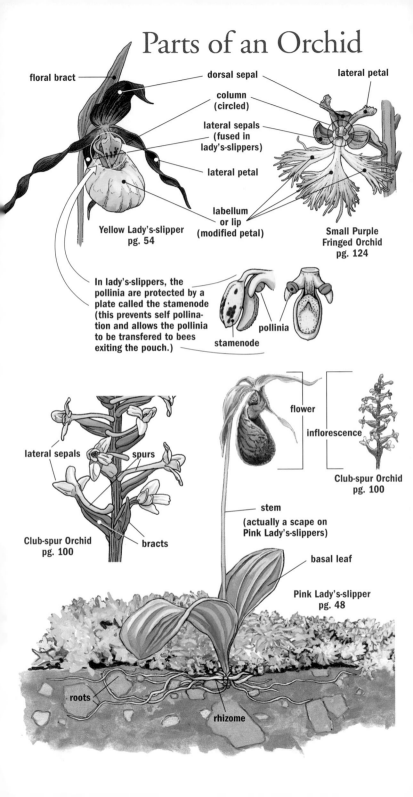

floral bract

dorsal sepal

lateral petal

column (circled)

lateral sepals (fused in lady's-slippers)

lateral petal

labellum or lip (modified petal)

Yellow Lady's-slipper pg. 54

Small Purple Fringed Orchid pg. 124

In lady's-slippers, the pollinia are protected by a plate called the stamenode (this prevents self pollination and allows the pollinia to be transfered to bees exiting the pouch.)

pollinia

stamenode

lateral sepals

spurs

Club-spur Orchid pg. 100

bracts

flower

inflorescence

Club-spur Orchid pg. 100

stem (actually a scape on Pink Lady's-slippers)

basal leaf

Pink Lady's-slipper pg. 48

roots

rhizome

the first leaves appear; the orchid is totally dependent on the fungus during this prolonged period.

All of the orchid species in New England and New York are terrestrial, with the possible exception of *Goodyera repens*, which sometimes grows in moss atop decaying tree trunks. Even at maturity most terrestrial orchids rely on a mycorrhizal relationship— in combination with photosynthesis—for a continued supply of minerals and carbohydrates. Coralroot orchids have no chlorophyll and hence are entirely dependent on their associated fungus for nutrients. Many scientists have described the orchid as a parasite on the fungus, but recent research shows that the symbiosis between the fungi and the orchid is mutual and reciprocal, with both benefiting from the exchange of nutrients. This fragile relationship with root fungi is what makes transplanting orchids from the wild very difficult, if not impossible. When the fungus dies, the orchid dies.

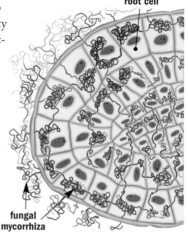

orchid root cell

fungal mycorrhiza

Illustration at a microscopic scale of fungal hyphae inside an orchid root tip. The mycorrhiza of the fungi provides nutrients to the developing orchid.

Orchid Seed Capsules

A ripened orchid ovary, or fruit, is classified as a capsule. The capsules are quite distinctive—due to their shape and position—and are useful as an identification tool. Orchid populations are oftentimes easier to locate in the winter, when the dried capsules are more visible against the snow.

Some orchid species—all *Listera* and several *Spiranthes* for example—release seed soon after fertilization while the stems are green and fleshy and do not form "woody" capsules that can be collected.

Collecting capsules is a benign way of keeping a memento of a beautiful and endangered group of plants—much better than digging or making pressed specimens. Many of the capsules pictured here are from the "pod" collection of orchid researcher Scott Shriver.

While not complete, the 43 species and varieties represented here exhibit the great range in morphology that can be found in orchid seed capsules. Some species—*Malaxis* and several *Spiranthes*—are greatly magnified to show detail. Happy winter orchid hunting!

*Amerorchis
rotundifolia*

*Aplectrum
hyemale*

*Arethusa
bulbosa*

*Calopogon
tuberosus*

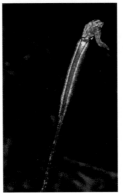

*Calypso
bulbosa*

*Coeloglossum
viride*

*Corallorhiza
maculata*

*Corallorhiza
odontorhiza*

*Cypripedium
acaule*

*Cypripedium
arietinum*

*Cypripedium
candidum*

var. *makasin*

*Cypripedium
parviflorum*

var. *pubescens*

*Cypripedium
parviflorum*

*Cypripedium
reginae*

*Epipactis
helleborine*

*Galearis
spectabilis*

*Goodyera
oblongifolia*

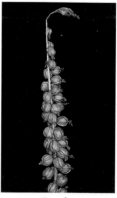

*Goodyera
pubescens*

*Goodyera
repens*

*Goodyera
tesselata*

*Isotria
verticillata*

*Liparis
liliifolia*

*Liparis
loeselii*

*Malaxis
monophylos*

*Malaxis
unifolia*

*Platanthera
blephariglottis*

*Platanthera
ciliaris*

*Platanthera
clavellata*

*Platanthera flava
var. herbiola*

*Platanthera
hookeri*

*Platanthera
lacera*

*Platanthera
macrophylla*

*Platanthera
orbiculata*

*Platanthera
pallida*

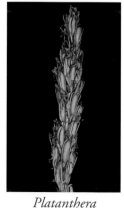

*Platanthera
psycodes*

*Pogonia
ophioglossoides*

*Spiranthes casei
var. casei*

*Spiranthes
cernua*

*Spiranthes lacera
var. gracilis*

*Spiranthes
ochroleuca*

*Spiranthes
tuberosa*

*Tipularia
discolor*

*Triphora
trianthophora*

Orchid Genera of New England & New York

The bird people have their act together—at least when it comes to standardization of common and scientific names. The world of botany could learn a thing or two from them. There is no single botanical organization that has the ability to standardize names. This leads to controversy and inconsistency in the naming of orchids and other plants. Systematics is the science of classifying organisms according to their phylogeny—their place on the evolutionary 'family tree' of life. Continually in flux as new discoveries cause changes in our understanding of plant relationships, systematics is best described as a snapshot of our knowledge at a particular moment in time. Accordingly, the list of orchid genera is continually changing as taxonomists discover, learn and debate plant relationships. Currently there are about 900 genera of orchids recognized worldwide. Below are the genera included in this book.

Amerorchis — Round-leaved Orchis

This generic name originates from two root words: *Amer* for American because it is a North American genus and *orchis* which is the Greek word for "testicle." *Amerorchis* is a single-species (monotypic) genus that was recently established in 1968. It was formerly included in the variable and widespread Old World genus *Orchis*, named for its two large round fleshy roots that resemble testicles. Some of the technical features used to separate *Amerorchis* from *Orchis* are the rhizomatous slender-fleshy roots rather than rounded tuberoids and the single basal leaf and scapose stem. The most recent data suggests that this species be included in the genus *Platanthera* but not all experts agree.

Orchis is also the root of the word "orchid" and the family name Orchidaceae. In classical Greek mythology Orchis, the son of a nymph and satyr, attempted to rape a priestess during a feast for Bacchus, the god of "wine." As punishment, Orchis was to be torn limb from limb by wild beasts but the gods intervened and his mutilated body was changed into a modest and slender plant with paired round tubers similar to the organs of his own undoing.

Aplectrum — Puttyroot

The genus name is derived from the Greek words *a*, meaning "without," and *plektron*, "spur" in reference to the spurless flowers. Although there are other orchids that have spurless flowers, this name was probably used to distinguish *Aplectrum* from *Tipularia* and *Calypso*—the other orchid genera with a single overwintering leaf. *Aplectrum* has only 2 species ascribed to it, *A. hyemale* and an additional one in Japan.

Arethusa — Dragon's-mouth

The genus is named after *Arethusa*, a beautiful river nymph in classical Greek mythology. Since this lovely orchid usually grows in wet habitats, it is aptly named. The genus includes only one species that is restricted to north-eastern North America, although in past years other orchid species have been incorrectly included in *Arethusa*, including one from Japan that is now placed in *Eleorchis*.

Dragon's-mouth

Queen bumblebees, reported as pollinators, are attracted to the yellow hairs on the lip. *Arethusa* flowers exhibit the syndrome known as the "false stamen" in which the lip, bearded with yellow, attracts bees but offers no pollen reward. Because it also offers little or no nectar, *Arethusa* is thought to be pollinated by inexperienced bumblebees, offering the promise of a meal, but giving no reward.

Some orchid experts speculate that *Arethusa* plants are relatively short-lived, compared to other terrestrial orchids; they seldom reproduce vegetatively and may depend on heavy seed production for survival. Blooming populations can fluctuate considerably at the same locality from year to year, but the reasons are not fully known.

Calopogon — Grass-Pinks

The genus name is from the Greek words *kalos* meaning "beautiful" and *pogon* meaning "beard" and refers to the yellow bristles on the lip of the flower. There are five species in this genus and all occur only in North America. New England and New York have one species.

The tuft of yellow-tipped hairs on the lip resembles pollen-filled anthers and attracts local bees and small butterflies. The lip is hinged at the base and when a bee lands on it, the lip collapses forward, and dumps the bee onto the column. This action forces the bee to make contact with the stigma and deposit any pollen it may have picked up from other flowers. As the confused bee leaves the flower, it picks up more sticky pollen and transports it to other calopogons as it continues its search for nectar.

Tuberous Grass-Pink (*Calopogon tuberosus*) has evolved into a master deceiver. A bee searching for pollen is attracted to pollenless yellow fringed hairs on the lip.

As the bee lands, the hinged lip collapses under the weight of the bee. This is one of only a few flowers that actually physically move their pollinator.

Calypso — Fairy Slipper

From the Greek *Kalypso*, the genus is named for the sea nymph Calypso, of Homer's *Odyssey*, who kept Ulysses hidden on her island for seven years. In Greek *calypso* means "hiding" or "concealment" referring to the plant's mystical beauty and clandestine haunts.

The genus consists of a single species, which is circumboreal. Four varieties have been described, only one of which has been found in New England and New York.

Calypso

Coeloglossum — Frog Orchid

Coeloglossum is a monotypic genus scattered across the entire Northern Hemisphere in suitable climates. Historically, the species we now include in *Coeloglossum* has been placed among several different genera. Sixty years ago, most botanists included it in the genus *Habenaria*, usually as *H. viridis* var. *bracteata*. Later, the species was transferred to *Coeloglossum* and now some botanists want to place it in *Dactylorhiza*. It seems that *Coeloglossum* is the odd Duck-billed Platypus of our native orchids; it does not seem to fit well in any genus.

Corallorhiza — Coralroots

The genus name *Corallorhiza* derives from the Greek word *korallion*—"coral" and *rhiza*—"root," referring to the coral-like appearance of the root in some species.

There are 13 species in the genus, which is widespread in North and Central America, with a center of distribution in Mexico. Seven species occur in the woods of the United States and Canada and one of these,

The bee falls back onto the column where it is coated with a sticky substance by the stigma. Further struggling causes pollen packets to adhere to the bee.

Upon escaping, the bee may pass on pollen from a previous Grass-Pink, or if this is his first visit to such a flower, then he may pollinate the next one visited.

Corallorhiza trifida, is circumboreal. There are 4 species and 3 varieties in New England and New York.

Coralroots are mycotropic plants—meaning that they derive all of their nourishment from green leafy plants through a complex relationship with specific mycorrhizal root-fungi acting as an intermediary. All orchids are mycotropic for at least part of their life-cycle, primarily during germination and early seedling growth. Many orchids eventually become self-supporting through photosynthesis. Most temperate zone terrestrial orchids maintain partial mycotropic dependence all of their lives, which is what makes transplanting and growing them so difficult; if the root-fungus dies, so do the orchids. Coralroots are nearly totally lacking in chlorophyll and are easily recognizable by their leafless stems, which display beautiful shades of brown, red and yellow and are characterized by small flowers that match the color of the stem. Two species (*C. odontorhiza* and *C. trifida*) contain trace amounts of chlorophyll and are able to photosynthesize minimally. The perennial coralloid rootstocks can remain dormant for years, producing

The underground rhizome's coral-like appearance gives rise to the common name (coralroot) and genus name (*Corallorhiza*).

blooming stems only when conditions are right for reproduction. Since they require no sunlight for photosynthesis, coralroots are able to thrive in the deepest, darkest woods.

Cypripedium — Lady's-slippers

The generic name *Cypripedium* is derived from two words: *Kypris* (Latinized as *Cypris*) the Greek goddess of love and beauty, and either

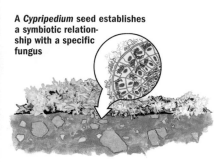

A *Cypripedium* seed establishes a symbiotic relationship with a specific fungus

A protocorm slowly develops underground, perhaps 3 to 7 years, living on starches provided by the fungi. Once it has grown a root system, a bud is produced.

It takes a dozen years or more for

the Latin word *pedis* meaning "foot" or the Greek word *pedilon* meaning "slipper." There are 45 to 50 species worldwide with 12 in North America; 5 species occur in New England and New York.

Cypripedium is one of the most alluring of all the orchid genera and its members are often the catalyst that first inspires a budding orchid enthusiast. The defining characteristic of the genus is the lip petal, which has evolved into a distinctive and very attractive pouch-shaped slipper. This lip looks and smells like an attractive food source but actually offers no nectar—utilizing deception to trap the pollinator that is unable to fly out of the small opening once it has entered the pouch. The insect eventually finds hairs that create a path past the stigma and one of the anthers to a pair of openings at the rear of the slipper. As it struggles to escape it first deposits any pollen it may have brought with it, and then comes in contact with the pollinia and a new mass of pollen which it carries away to the next flower visited, achieving cross-pollination. Unfortunately the various species of bees that are the pollinators soon learn of this deception and avoid lady's-slippers; thus the plants have to rely on young, inexperienced bees, greatly limiting the chance of pollination. Luckily, the plants also reproduce vegetatively by sending up shoots from horizontally creeping rhizomes, which creates the large colonies that cause the nature lover to pause and stand in awe.

Most are slow growing and can require a decade or more to reach flowering size. Large colonies—often with dozens of flowering stems—can be one hundred or more years old. Advances in commercial propagation of *Cypripedium* have been made in recent years and most species are now available from mail-order nurseries, leaving absolutely no reason to dig wild plants, unless they are threatened by development.

Of the 4 species found in New England and New York, 3 are easily differentiated. But classification of the yellow lady's-slipper complex has

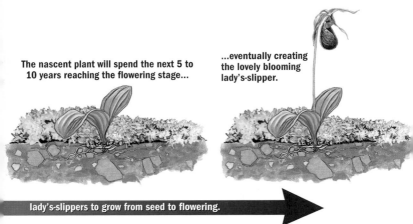

The nascent plant will spend the next 5 to 10 years reaching the flowering stage...

...eventually creating the lovely blooming lady's-slipper.

lady's-slippers to grow from seed to flowering.

challenged botanists ever since Linnaeus first described the genus in 1753. *Cypripedium calceolus* was described in his *Species Plantarum* as the type for the genus, and this was the Latin name that the Yellow Lady's-slipper—a circumboreal plant—was known by for the next 200+ years, with the North American plants usually being considered a variety or varieties of *C. calceolus*. A bewildering array of synonyms exist for the species and show how challenging it was for early botanists to classify the varieties of yellow lady's-slippers found across North America. In the late 20th century contemporary investigators split *Cypripedium calceolus* into two taxa, calling the plants found in North America *Cypripedium parviflorum*, the name given by British botanist Richard Salisbury to a specimen he collected in Virginia in 1791. To him it was obviously different from *C. calceolus* and warranted species status. In addition, a distinct subset has been split off into a separate species, *Cypripedium kentuckiense*. In an attempt to further clarify the taxonomy of a confusing species, 4 varieties of *C. parviflorum* have been named; 3 are found in New England and New York. Variations in climate, habitat and soil types produce many subtle differences within each variety and hybridization can occur in populations of mixed varieties, further confusing the issue.

Because most herbarium records in New England and New York have yet to be updated in regards to the recently named varieties of *C. parviflorum*, only one map for that species is provided, without regard to variety. Further range information is given within each varietal description.

Dactylorhiza (see *Coeloglossum*)

Epipactis — Helleborines

Epipactis is a genus of approximately 25 species found primarily in temperate Eurasia. Three species occur in North America: *E. gigantea* is native to western USA, *E. atrorubens* is apparently naturalized in Vermont but has not been recently observed, and *E. helleborine* is introduced from Europe.

Epipacits is the name given by Theophrastes, an ancient Greek philosopher and botanist, to a plant capable of curdling milk, which may or may not have been from this genus. The plant for which *Epipactis* was named may have been a helleborine in the genus *Helleborus*, a member of the Buttercup Family; however, the resemblance may have been based on ancient medicinal uses, rather than appearance.

Galearis — Showy Orchis

The name *Galearis* is derived from the Latin *galea*, meaning "helmet" in reference to the helmet-like hood formed by the two lateral petals and three sepals. Only 2 species are currently included in the genus: *G. spectabilis* from eastern North America and *G. cyclochila* from Asia. A century ago, both *G. spectabilis* and *Amerorchis rotundifolia* were considered to be American representatives of the European genus *Orchis*, but recent DNA studies confirm that the three genera are distinct.

Goodyera repens

Goodyera — Rattlesnake-Plantains

Origin of the name: *Goodyera* was named in 1813 for the famed English botanist John Goodyear (1592–1664). The common name, rattlesnake orchid, refers to the beautifully marked and reticulated leaves, which attract more attention than do the flowers. These attractive leaves have earned the genus the name of "jewel orchids" in Asia. The flowers are small, and a magnifying lens is needed to appreciate the unique teapot-like shape of the lip. There are about 40 species worldwide, with four in North America; all four occur in New England and New York.

Goodyera tesselata

Goodyera pubescens

Because the leaves resemble those of Common Plantain (*Plantago*) they are often called 'plantain orchids'. They are also called 'rattlesnake orchids' due to the fact that the early European settlers in North America used their leaves to treat snakebite, because the leaves

Goodyera oblongifolia

resemble the skin of a rattlesnake. This was in accordance with their ancient belief in the "doctrine of signatures." The leaves were chewed by some North American aboriginal women to ease pain during childbirth.

The plants in this genus are characterized by a horizontally creeping rhizome, which produce roots at intervals. At the rhizome's terminus, the rosette of attractive evergreen leaves variously marked with silvery white is produced. Most can be identified by their leaves (see sidebar photos). The rosette dies after flowering, leaving younger clones elsewhere on the rhizome. Consequently, compact colonies often develop.

Goodyera is technically a difficult group and in many ways is comparable to the related *Spiranthes*. No one characteristic suffices to distinguish between the species and multiple characteristics have to be considered for reliable identification. Hybridization is rampant wherever two or more *Goodyera* species grow in proximity with each other. Populations which cannot be attributed to any one of the typical species are sometimes encountered and no attempt has been made to name any of them as they are so variable.

Gymnadeniopsis (see *Platanthera*)

Isotria — Whorled Pogonias

The genus name is from the Greek *isos*, meaning "equal" and *tria*, meaning "three" referring to the three sepals which are of equal size and shape. Plants of this genus are characterized by a whorl of five or six leaves at the top of the hollow stem. This peculiar, umbrella-like arrangement of leaves is unique in the orchid family. One or rarely two flowers are borne above the leaves and the lip is conspicuously tuberculate-crested. Pollinators are unknown.

Closely related to the genus *Pogonia*, and formerly placed in it by some botanists, *Isotria* includes only two species and both are restricted to the eastern United States and adjacent Canada. Immature or sterile plants are sometimes confused with *Medeola virginiana*, the Indian Cucumber-Root (see photo on page 75). Examination of the stems reveals that those of *Medeola* are thin, minutely hairy, and solid, whereas those of *Isotria* are stouter, smooth, and hollow.

Liparis — Twayblades

The genus name is derived from the Greek *liparos* meaning "fat" or "greasy" in reference to the oily look and feel of the leaves. The names *Liparis* and lipid (another word for fat) are both derived from the same basic root. The genus, closely related to *Malaxis*, is commonly referred to as the false-twayblades to distinguish it from the genus *Listera*, the twayblades. The leaves of *Liparis* are basal and erect; the leaves of *Listera* are nearly horizontal about halfway up the stem. *Liparis* includes about 250 species worldwide with 3 species in North America, 2 of which occur in our region.

Listera — Twayblades

Origin of the name: The genus is named for the English naturalist Martin Lister (1638–1711). It is a circumboreal genus with 25 members; 7 species occur in North America with 4 found in New England and New York. The common name, twayblade—tway meaning two—is also shared by the genus *Liparis*, the so-called false twayblades. The two genera can be easily differentiated by the placement of the two leaves on the stem; in *Liparis* they are found at the very base of the stem, in *Listera* they grow at a point about one-third to halfway up the stem. Recent molecular studies have suggested that *Listera*, although at first sight different in appearance, be placed in the Old World genus *Neottia*—formerly a one-species genus—as the two genera belong to a poly-phyletic (sharing a common ancestor) group and are closely related. Research regarding North American *Listera* species is ongoing and not yet finalized; for that reason the name *Listera* will be used in this publication.

Listera australis

Listera auriculata

Listera convallarioides

Listera are small orchids, often only a few inches tall and rarely reaching the ten-inch mark. All have a pair of opposite leaves that lack any stalk, which occur one-third to halfway up the stem. The stem has a few sheathing bracts near its base and becomes somewhat pubescent above the leaves. The flowers are usually fairly numerous and are loosely arranged on the upper portion of the stem. Sepals and petals tend to be proportion-

Listera cordata

ately small, the lip unusually large. The flowers are prominently forked or two-lobed; use of a hand lens is required to best see the detail of these fascinating flowers.

Our *Listera* species are easily distinguished by lip shape (see illustrations).

Listera has a very interesting pollination mechanism and is another orchid species that attracted the attention of Darwin. Pressure sensitive hairs located at the base of the rostellum act as a trigger for pollination and only the slightest nudge from the back of a pollinator will trigger the contrivance. A droplet of quick-drying glue is ejected onto a visiting insect that touches one of the hairs, and the pollinia are released to fall on the glue. Once the pollinia have been removed the spread rostellum remains as a protective cover of the stigma for approximately 1 day, after which it gradually lifts, exposing the stigma. Visiting insects are then able to deposit pollinia, completing the pollination process. This elaborate procedure virtually ensures cross-pollination and demonstrates one of the many specializations of orchids. The flowers persist for some time after pollination, much to the delight of orchid lovers. The seeds are also expelled from the capsule by forceful action.

Malaxis — Adder's-mouths

Malaxis is a large genus with 250 to 300 species worldwide and is most diverse in Asia and the East Indies. Fifteen species occur in North America north of Mexico; 3 species are found in New England and New York.

The name, *Malaxis*, is derived from the Greek word *malaxis*, meaning "a softening," in reference to the soft, succulent consistency of the leaves.

In many species the sepals and petals pull back, pushing the lip and pollen-bearing column forward. This gives the plants a look resembling the mouth and tongue of a snake, inspiring the common name 'Adder's-mouth'.

Like the closely related False Twayblades, the Adder's-Mouths are not showy and are a challenge to the field botanist, due to their small size and relative rarity. The flowers are some of the smallest of the Orchidaceae; many are not more than a few millimeters in any dimension. All species have a pseudobulbous stem, which is more corm-like in the temperate climate species.

Platanthera — Rein-, Bog-, Fringed-, and Round-leaved Orchids

The name, *Platanthera*, is derived from two Greek words: *platys*—"wide, broad" and *anther*—"anther" referring to the unusually wide anther. It is comprised of about 200 species of terrestrial orchids that are found in temperate regions of the eastern and western hemispheres. It is also

Club-spur Orchid: as the flowers develop they twist about 180 degrees—some a little more and some a little less.

the largest genus in New England and New York with 18 species and is extremely varied.

A confusing genus, *Platanthera* was originally placed in the large primarily tropical genus *Habenaria*, whose name is from the Latin word *habena*—"rein," or "strap." It has been split into several segregate genera in recent years. In contrast to *Habenaria*, which is characterized by its thick, tuberous roots and two-parted petals, *Platanthera* has fleshy roots without tubers and undivided petals.

Some sections in this widely varied genus are well defined, others are not. Four of the well defined are: the **rein-orchids**, which are named for their strap-like lip that resembles reins; the **bog orchids**, named for their choice of habitat; the **round-leaved orchids**, named for their fleshy, over-sized leaves which make them some of the more bizarre looking of our orchid species; and the famous **fringed-orchids**, with their colorful, showy flowers in tall spikes or racemes, which are named for their large and often colorful fringed lip petal, and are amongst our region's "trophy" species. Fringed-orchids are divided into two groups: those with an entire or undivided lip and those with a three-lobed lip.

Rose Pogonia

Platanthera species grow in a wide range of soil types and habitats, from strongly basic soils to deeply acidic bog soils, from wetlands and forest openings to open tundra; the one requirement of most species is moist soil.

Pogonia — Pogonia Orchids

In the late 1800s, *Pogonia* was considered a more diverse genus than it is today. At that time, 4 orchid species from our region were included in the genus: the Rose Pogonia, Three Birds Orchid and the Large and Small Whorled Pogonias. Another species, the majestic and beautiful Spreading Pogonia (*Cleistes divaricata*), known from just south of our range, also was once included in *Pogonia*. As currently circumscribed, there is only one species of *Pogonia* endemic to North America, *Pogonia ophioglossoides*; a similar species, *P. japonica*, occurs in China and Japan.

The occurrence of *Calopogon* with *Pogonia* is apparently of particular benefit to *Calopogon*, as it exploits pollinators that visit the similar-looking *Pogonia*. *Pogonia* offers pollinator reinforcement by providing nectar, whereas *Calopogon* does not; but naïve bees do not know the difference.

Spiranthes — Ladies'-Tresses

The genus name is derived from two Greek words: *speira* "coil," and *anthos* "flower," in reference to the coiled or spiraled appearance of the flower spike. Some of the most beautiful of our "miniature" orchids, the gracefully spiraled, jewel-like blossoms of the genus have a crystalline appearance when magnified. The common name alludes to the resemblance of the flower spike to braided hair, suggesting the ancient art of braiding flowers into the hair of maidens, or even a maiden's bodice. Most *Spiranthes* species are the last orchids of the season to bloom and are a vital component of the autumn pageant in our region. The basal leaves are often withered or absent at blooming time.

Spiranthes is a cosmopolitan genus comprised of about 50 species worldwide, with 26 found in North America, including 8 in New England and New York. Easily recognizable, the genus includes some of the more difficult species of orchids to identify; intermediate forms and hybrids challenge our never-ending attempt to neatly classify the natural world.

Tipularia — Crane-fly Orchid

The genus name is from *Tipula*, the genus of insects to which the crane-flies belong, because of the resemblance of the straggly long-spurred flowers to crippled crane-flies in flight. This genus consists of 3 similar species isolated from each other in the far reaches of the world: *Tipularia josephi* in the Himalayan Mountains, *T. japonica* in Japan, and *T. discolor* in the eastern United States.

In many respects, the life history of *Tipularia* is like that of Puttyroot—*Aplectrum*. It produces a single over-wintering leaf in September that disappears the following spring, and it sends up a leaf-less flowering stalk during the growing season. *Aplectrum*, however, is a spring bloomer, while *Tipularia* blooms in summer.

Triphora — Three Birds Orchid

Approximately 20 species comprise this New World genus. In North America only *Triphora trianthophora* extends northward beyond the subtropical climate of Florida. All arise from swollen, tuberous roots and some produce colorful, although small, flowers. Several species have flowers that do not open.

The name, *Triphora*, is derived from two Greek words: *tri*—"three-fold," and *phoros*—"bearing," referring to the number of flowers, often three, or to the three crests on the three-lobed lip.

Triphora was long known as a member of the genus *Pogonia*, but is not as closely allied as originally thought, due to differences in column morphology and features of the pollinia.

Orchid Photography
by Tom Nelson

For many people, the joy of photographing a rare and elusive native orchid species is almost as exciting as the thrill of discovering it secreted away in an impenetrable bog or remote boreal forest. Recent improvements in digital technology have made it possible for anyone to take reasonably good images with the simple push of a button, but for high-quality

work, certain equipment is a must. High-end digital cameras do amazing things and certainly have many advantages, but I prefer the look, technical simplicity and color accuracy —especially when photographing red and pink flowers—of film, and all of my images are shot in that medium.

Over the last five years of serious orchid hunting I have learned and adopted some fail-proof techniques for obtaining good plant images— digital or film—in the field.

For orchid "portraits" using natural light, a tripod is essential. High-priced models are available that lie flat on the ground; I modified my cheaper one to do the same thing by

A lens-mounted ring flash and extension tubes are important orchid photography accessories. Also clothes that can get dirty!

simply removing the center column with a hack saw. The winning combination for a great image is: a tripod with either a 50 mm or 105 mm macro lens; an aperture setting of F32 combined with a slow shutter speed— often as slow as ½ second for maximum depth of field—and of course the obligatory shutter release cable.

Use of a reflector is a good way to light up dark areas. The final touch for me is a black background for heightened subject definition; I use custom-made black velvet backgrounds of different dimensions that conveniently roll up to avoid wrinkling and for easier transport.

Wind and glaring sun are the nemeses of all plant photographers and there are several solutions to this problem. White diffusion umbrellas (I always carry two) provide an even suffusion of light over the subject— especially in the dappled shade of woodland settings—and provide some wind protection as well. But to really solve the problem, wildflower photographers have long used diffusion, or light tents. They are now conveniently commercially available over the Internet and are a great addition to any serious flower photographer's arsenal. I have customized mine with the addition of a black velvet background. The tent—made out of white parachute cloth—not only baths the subject in a wonderful "overcast" light, but it also stabilizes tall, top-heavy orchids by eliminating wind.

Slow shutter speeds can then be utilized to create stunning orchid portraits. A reflector can be placed inside to provide fill lighting. In the past I had tried twist-tying the subjects to wooden stakes, a method employed by others, but found it to be too cumbersome and time consuming.

Since many species of orchids grow in dark bogs and forests, flash is an essential tool. For close-up work, the use of a lens-mounted ring flash—usually with one or two extension tubes for magnification—is essential. The flash allows the photographer to "grab" shots without a tripod. The results at f32 can be revelatory; details of tiny orchid flowers emerge, as if from another world; floral details unavailable to the naked eye are presented well-lighted and in sharp focus.

When using ring flash in bright sun, a diffusion umbrella should be utilized for optimum results. Precise focusing is the key; with the macro lens fully extended and elbows planted firmly on the ground acting as a "human tripod," I move the camera mere millimeters for optimum focus.

Top: White umbrellas diffuse strong sun to make a softer, more pleasing light.
Middle: A portable black velvet backdrop allows the orchid to stand out from a cluttered background.
Bottom: A homemade diffusion tent softens strong light and keeps the wind at bay.

This technique does require getting "down and dirty" in close proximity to the plants, often with one's left ear in the muck to stabilize the camera. When in this prone position one is of course consorting with myriad bugs; good bug spray, long sleeves and mosquito hat as well as a post-photo-session "tick-check" are all mandatory. I always try to inflict minimal collateral damage on surrounding plants and check photo sites carefully before "bedding down."

Have fun!

How to use this Field Guide

Orchids of the New England & New York is designed to make field identification easier for you, the reader. Through the use of color photos of
the entire plant, close ups of individual flowers, rare or unusual color
forms, seed capsules and leaves, we have created a unique guide that
highlights the orchid traits you are most likely to see in the field and
need for proper identification. Detailed range maps help you narrow
your search. This handy, compact and easy-to-use guide is small enough
to tuck into any daypack.

Coverage

About 65 species/varieties of native orchids occur in New England
(abbreviated **NE**) and New York (**NY**). We cover them all, but lump
some extremely similar species/subspecies into a single two-page spread.
Under *Abundance* we abbreviate the other states as **RI** (Rhode Island),
MA (Massachusetts), **CT** (Connecticut), **VT** (Vermont), **NH** (New
Hampshire) and **ME** (Maine).

Names

Latin and common names are given for all species. Even botanists and
their professional organizations don't agree on common names (and
even genera placement) of our native orchids. The authors have used
the most widely accepted names from other published sources. *Other
Names* lists alternative names; colloquial and regional, while *Name
Origin* explains the etymology of the Latin/scientific name.

Seed Capsules

This may be the first book in history to show color photos of the capsules of many of the northeastern orchid species. And because orchid
hunting doesn't have to end when the blooming does, these photos will
be a useful tool.

Phenograms

The red bar phenograms show when the range of flowering dates for
that species. Peak flowering dates are likely in the middle of the red bar,
but remember that microhabitats, latitude and elevation can vary bloom
phenology for individual species by days to weeks, especially in a region
as large and diverse as New England and New York.

Habitat

Our region enjoys a wide variety of habitats due to geological features,
latitude and elevation. It's this variety of bogs, fens, meadows, seeps,
swamps and forests that allow orchids to thrive, each in their own, often
highly specialized, niche. Below the phenogram we list the favored habitats of that orchid.

Range

Broad, brief, descriptions describe North American distribution.

Nature Notes

Fascinating snippets of natural history are included here. Also we include interesting facets of insect pollination.

Range Maps

A very detailed map of the seven state area (including county lines) shows the range of that species. **One red dot means the species has been recorded in that county, but does not differentiate between historical and current records.** All dots are based on herbarium voucher collections. If a species is officially designated "extirpated" within a state, this will be noted in red under the *Abundance* header. Our knowledge of species' ranges changes daily and yearly as new populations are discovered and others disappear. Report sightings of out-of-range orchids to a local university.

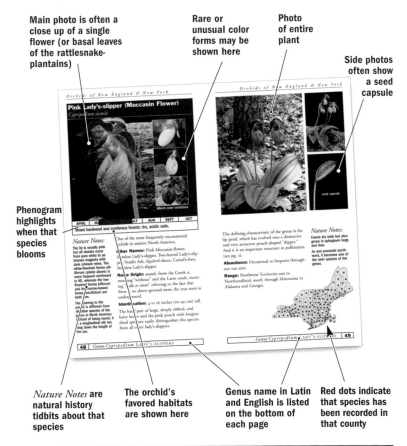

Main photo is often a close up of a single flower (or basal leaves of the rattlesnake-plantains)

Rare or unusual color forms may be shown here

Photo of entire plant

Side photos often show a seed capsule

Phenogram highlights when that species blooms

Nature Notes **are natural history tidbits about that species**

The orchid's favored habitats are shown here

Genus name in Latin and English is listed on the bottom of each page

Red dots indicate that species has been recorded in that county

Small Round-leaf Orchid
Amerorchis rotundifolia

APRIL	MAY	JUNE	JULY	AUG	SEPT	OCT

Restricted to shaded calcareous bogs, usually with N. White Cedar, *Thuja occidentalis*, and other conifers. The frail roots cannot tolerate heat or acid.

Nature Notes:

This species will undoubtedly be profoundly affected by climate change since it requires cool temperatures to survive.

The pollinator remains unknown; the plant probably relies upon self-pollination and vegetative reproduction.

Like snowflakes, no two flowers of *Amerorchis* are alike in terms of the spotting pattern.

Can be abundant in spots.

A lucky find in our area; it is one of the most photogenic of our native orchids.

Other Names: One-leaf Orchid, Round-leaved Orchis/Orchid.

Name Origin: The name, *rotundifolia*, is a Latin word meaning "round-leaved" referring to the round shape of the solitary leaf characteristic of the species.

Identification: 3 to 14 inches (7–35 cm) tall.

When in flower it is impossible to confuse this plant with any other orchid. The white lip—with its red to purple "peppermint" spots—is unique amongst North American orchids. A non-blooming plant can be distinguished from the similar *Platanthera obtusata*—another one-leaved species of similar proportions—by the shape of its leaf, which is widest at the middle;

forma immaculata

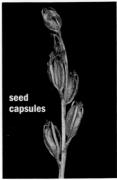
forma lineata

seed capsules

Six different color forms have been named so far. In forma *lineata* the spots on the flower are replaced by large splotches of color that look like they were painted by Van Gogh; the white-lipped form (forma *immaculata*) lacks any spots and has a pure white lip and petals (see photos above).

the leaf of the blunt-leaved rein orchid is widest beyond the middle.

Abundance: Very rare and local in northern Maine. Extirpated in New Hampshire, Vermont and New York.

Range: Alaska east to Newfoundland and Greenland, south to Montana and Wyoming, northern portions of Great Lakes states from Minnesota east to Maine. It is more abundant in the northern portions of its range.

Putty Root (Adam-and-Eve)
Aplectrum hyemale

| APRIL | MAY | JUNE | JULY | AUG | SEPT | OCT |

Rich deciduous woods, especially those dominated by beech and Sugar Maple.

Nature Notes:

Puttyroot is also known as the Adam-and-Eve Orchid, due to the presence of two underground corms on each plant. In the old days poor people in the Southern States would wear the corms as amulets and tell each other's fortunes by placing the separated bulbs in water and as "Adam or Eve" popped up, calculate future events.

Easiest to locate in late autumn, or during a snowless period in the winter.

Self-fertilization, asexual seed formation without fertilization and vegetative reproduction are the norm.

An unusual orchid with a September to May growth cycle. After flowering, the plant lies dormant through the summer.

Other Names: Eve-and-Adam.

Name Origin: Derived from the Latin word *hyems*, "winter" referring to the habit of the plant producing a single winter leaf.

Identification: 7 to 20 inches (18–50 cm) tall.

Puttyroot's most distinctive feature is its large blue-green basal leaf. It could be confused with coralroots, which also have a leafless stem. Puttyroot contains chlorophyll and hence has a greenish stem; coralroots have a yellowish or reddish stem. In *forma pallidum*, the stems and flowers are yellow and the lip unspotted.

Aplectrum, like *Calypso* and *Tipularia*, has the

The single rounded blue-green basal leaf is Puttyroot's most distinctive feature.

seed pods

curious trait of having an alternative vegetative lifecycle; instead of having a growing season from spring to autumn, as do most plants, its season is autumn to spring. The single over-winter leaf appears in the autumn and conducts photosynthesis during the winter thereby avoiding competition for light during the normal growing season. The leaf fades shortly before the emergence of the flowering stalk in early to mid-May.

Abundance: Very rare in NE & NY.

Range: Minnesota east to southern Ontario and Vermont, south to northern South Carolina and west to eastern Oklahoma.

Nature Notes:

The corms of Puttyroot are said to have been used by early settlers to glue together broken pieces of china, hence the name.

Dragon's-mouth (Arethusa)
Arethusa bulbosa

APRIL	MAY	JUNE	JULY	AUG	SEPT	OCT

Sphagnum bogs, coniferous swamps, calcareous fens, moist acid sandy meadows.

Nature Notes:

During the past 100 years, *Arethusa* has vanished from many localities throughout NE & NY, largely because of human activities.

Individuals bearing two flowers are a special reward for the persistent native orchid enthusiast.

Two unusual color forms have been described: the white-flowered forma *albiflora* and the lilac-blue flowered forma *subcaerulea*.

Dragon's-mouth is seldom observed because it prefers habitats that are difficult to get to.

The name Dragon's-mouth conjures up images of a fiery-red, water dragon emerging from the mist of a prehistoric swamp.

Other Names: Swamp-pink, Wild Pink, Bog Pink, Bog Rose, Moss Nymph.

Name Origin: *Arethusa*, from the Greek, means "the waterer;" *bulbosa*, from the Latin, means "bulbed" referring to the bulb-like corm.

Identification: 4 to 12 inches (10–30 cm) tall.

Often grows with Grass-pink and Rose Pogonia, but the flowers differ dramatically in shape. The absence of a leaf at flowering time also distinguishes Dragon's-mouth from the other pink orchids that bloom at the same time in similar habitats.

rare white form

Abundance: Rare and declining. Population size often varies greatly from year to year.

Range: Southern Manitoba east to Newfoundland, Minnesota south to northern Indiana and northern South Carolina.

Nature Notes:

This species is one of the very few orchids whose original scientific name, dating back to 1753, has remained unchanged.

Dragon's-mouth is one of our most beautiful native wildflowers.

Lilac-colored flower of forma *subcaerula*

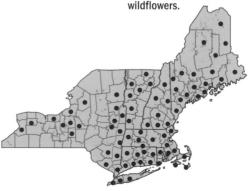

Tuberous Grass-Pink
Calopogon tuberosus var. tuberosus

lilac-flowered form

APRIL	MAY	JUNE	JULY	AUG	SEPT	OCT

Bogs, fens, peatlands, and open coniferous swamps.

Nature Notes:

For many years this species was known as *Calopogon pulchellus* and many orchid books published before 1965 used that incorrect name.

Grass-pink flowers over a long period of time, with only a few flowers open at the same time.

Variety *latifolius* has been described from the open heathlands of northern Maine but is no longer considered to be worthy of taxonomic recognition.

Peculiar among our orchids because the flowers are non-resupinate ("upside down").

Other Names: Grass-pink, Common Grass-pink, Grass-pink Orchid, Pretty Calopogon.

Name Origin: *Calopogon*, from the Greek *kalos*, meaning "beautiful" and *pogon* meaning "beard," hence "beautiful beard" referring to the colorful tuft of bristles on the lip. And *tuberosus*, from the Latin, meaning "tubered" referring to the tuberous corms.

Identification: 8 to 22 inches (20–55 cm) tall.

The non-resupinate flower is distinctive and easily distinguishes the genus. Each plant has usually one erect, grass-like leaf when in prime bloom.

Abundance: Locally common throughout.

seed capsules

Range: Found from Newfoundland south to Florida, west to southeastern Manitoba and eastern Texas. It also occurs in Cuba and the Bahamas.

Nature Notes:

White-flowered forms are known as forma *albiflorus.*

Large colonies of several hundred plants can be found throughout the region.

Calypso (Eastern Fairy-Slipper)
Calypso bulbosa var. americana

APRIL	MAY	JUNE	JULY	AUG	SEPT	OCT

Cool calcareous coniferous woodlands, usually with N. White Cedar.

Nature Notes:

The bumblebee pollinator is lured by the yellow hairs that it thinks contain nectar (there is none) or pollen. Pollen sticks to the bee's back where it can't reach it and when it enters another flower, the pollen touches the even stickier female part of the flower and pollination is achieved.

Very few of our native orchids possess the sheer beauty and loveliness of Calypso. This elusive jewel-like orchid is much-sought-after and rarely found.

Other Names: Venus's Slipper, Angel Slipper, Deer's-head Orchid, Hider-of-the-North, Redwood Orchid.

Name Origin: Derived from the Latin word *bulbosa*, in reference to the bulb-like corm.

Identification: 2 to 9 inches (5–22 cm) tall.

Calypso is very different from other orchids and has no close relatives. The single dark green, satiny leaf appears in late summer and withers shortly after flowering begins in the spring. A single (rarely two) flower of unsurpassed beauty droops from the end of the stem; its jewel-like marvels are best appreciated

seed capsule

forma *rosea*

Rare white flowered forma *albiflora*

There are two color forms: the white forma *albiflora* and the pink forma *rosea*.

from the "worm's-eye view" i.e. lying flat on the forest floor. The distinctive slipper is a marvel to behold: the lip-sac is vividly marked on the inner surface with reddish-brown spots and lines and expands forward into a white apron which is attractively bearded with golden-yellow hairs spotted with purple. The frost-resistant flower scape emerges to become one of the earliest spring flowers, also setting it apart from all other orchids in New England and New York.

Abundance: Rare and local in northern Maine and Vermont.
Extirpated in New Hampshire and New York.

Range: Occurs from Alaska east to Newfoundland, south in the Rocky Mountains to New Mexico and Arizona, south to the upper Great Lakes region and northern New England.

Long-bracted Orchid
Coeloglossum viride var. virescens

| APRIL | MAY | JUNE | JULY | AUG | SEPT | OCT |

Rich, moist, often shady hardwood and coniferous woodlands

Nature Notes:

Many varieties and sub-species have been described during the past 200 years, but currently only two varieties are generally recognized: the predominately Eurasian var. *viride* and the widespread North American var. *virescens*.

North American individuals of this species can be distinguished from the Eurasian var. *viride* by the very long, spreading floral bracts that greatly exceed the flowers.

The floral bracts are leaf-like and conspicuous, especially in the lower part of the spike, where they exceed the flowers by several lengths.

Some orchid experts include this species in the genus *Dactylorhiza*, but other experts continue to recognize the two genera as separate but closely related.

Other Names: Frog Orchid, Long-bracted Frog Orchid, American Frog Orchid, Long-bracted Green Orchid, Bracted Bog Orchid, Satyr Orchid.

Name Origin: *Coeloglossum*, from the Greek *koilos*, meaning "hollow" and *glossa* meaning "tongue" referring to the nectary extending below the base of the lip; *viride*, from the Latin *viridis*, meaning "green" referring to the greenish flowers and foliage.

Identification: 6 to 18 inches (15–45 cm) tall.

This species superficially resembles *Platanthera flava* var. *herbiola* in the field and dried herbar-

ium specimens are distinguished only by very careful examination. The lip of the former is tridentate whereas the lip of the later is blunt, with a central tubercle.

Abundance: Occasional and scattered; more common in calcareous woodlands, usually in the cooler parts of the region; often along roadsides and trails.

Range: Alaska east to Newfoundland, south to Washington, New Mexico, Iowa, and North Carolina.

Nature Notes:

The floral parts remain on the plant long after pollination, making it appear still in flower many weeks after blooming.

Spotted Coralroot
Corallorhiza maculata var. maculata
Corallorhiza maculata var. occidentalis

C. *maculata* var. *maculata*

| APRIL | MAY | JUNE | JULY | AUG | SEPT | OCT |

Shady deciduous and coniferous woods.

Nature Notes:

Dr. John Freudenstein completed a comprehensive study of the species in 1997 and split it into three varieties: var. *maculata*, var. *mexicana*, and var. *occidentalis*. Later, a fourth variety was described: var. *ozettensis*. Two of these varieties occur in NE & NY.

Spotted Coralroot is believed to be pollinated by small bees.

Flowering time: Variety *maculata*: late June to August; variety *occidentalis*: 1 to 4 weeks earlier than var. *maculata*—late May to July.

A brightly colored and highly variable orchid that requires no sunlight for photosynthesis and is able to thrive in the deepest, darkest woods.

Other Names: Large Coral-root, Summer Coralroot.

Name Origin: The species and varietal name *maculata* is from the Latin word *macula* meaning "spot," and refers to the spotted lip. The varietal name *occidentalis* is Latin for "western."

Identification: 6 to 26 inches (15–66 cm) tall.

The two varieties are most easily distinguished by the width and shape of the lip and the difference in blooming times. Variety *maculata* has a tall and slender growth form and is characterized by fewer flowers displayed in a more open inflorescence. The flowers have a rectangular lip with parallel sides and it blooms later.

C. maculata var. occidentalis

C. maculata var. maculata

flower buds

seed capsules

Variety *occidentalis* is a more robust plant with a denser inflorescence and a tendency to grow in clumps; the lip is broadly rounded at the tip, and it blooms earlier. The two varieties are sometimes found growing together. In NE & NY, the most common form has a flesh-colored stem, sepals and petals and a white lip with red spots.

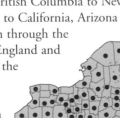

Color forms are varied; Here is a yellow form with an unspotted lip.

Abundance: Variety *maculata* is one of the most common orchids in NE & NY; variety *occidentalis* is less common.

Range: Widespread. British Columbia to Newfoundland, south in the mountains to California, Arizona and New Mexico; south through the Great Lakes and New England and then along the spine of the Appalachians to northern Georgia and South Carolina. Also found in Mexico and Central America.

This map combines the range of both varieties.

Autumn Coralroot
Corallorhiza odontorhiza var. odontorhiza

Pringle's Autumn Coralroot
Corallorhiza odontorhiza var. pringlei

APRIL	MAY	JUNE	JULY	AUG	SEPT	OCT

Rich deciduous woods, mostly Beech-Sugar Maple, damp or dry soils, or occasionally sandy soils. Sometimes favors recently disturbed areas.

Nature Notes:

Very difficult to locate in autumn woods because of its small size and coloration which is very similar to that of the fallen leaves. The diminutive *C. odontorhiza* is an interesting orchid well worth seeking out. Dr. John Freudenstein's research shows that *C. odontorhiza* var. *pringlei* is the "typical" form of the species and will not set fruit unless pollinated by an insect, a less than guaranteed proposition. Variety *odontorhiza* has overcome a seeming lack of pollinators by evolving self-pollinating flowers.

Often called the "ugly duckling" of the coralroots, this fascinating, hard-to-spot species has an unusual autumnal blooming cycle.

Other Names: Late Coralroot, Fall Coralroot, Small-flowered Coralroot.

Name Origin: Derived from the Greek word *odonto*—"tooth" and *rhiza*—"root," referring to the tooth-like appearance of the swollen base of the stem. Variety *pringlei* is named for botanist Cyrus Pringle (1838–1911) who discovered approximately 1,200 new species of plants.

Identification: 4 to 11 inches (10–28 cm) tall.

Because of its autumnal blooming-time, this species cannot be confused with any other coralroot. The two varieties are sometimes found within the same population, but are differentiated by the presence of (or lack of) a

seed
capsules

well-developed lip. Variety *odontorhiza* is variable and can have somewhat opened flowers, but they are much different in lip proportions than the well-developed, broader lip of var. *pringlei*. The ovaries are inflated and well developed at blooming time.

Abundance: Widespread but never common, it is a southern species that reaches the northern limit of its range in southern NE & NY. Two varieties occur in NE & NY: var. *odontorhiza*, which has self-fertilizing flowers that do not open, and the less-common var. *pringlei* that has open, insect-pollinated flowers.

Range: Nebraska east to Maine, south to northern Florida and eastern Texas.

Striped Coralroot
Corallorhiza striata var. striata

| APRIL | MAY | JUNE | JULY | AUG | SEPT | OCT |

Mixed and coniferous forests, favoring areas near limestone. It requires cool soil to survive.

Nature Notes:

The largest and showiest of the North American coralroots, the ruby red blossoms of striped coralroot are exquisitely beautiful.

The plants can form impressive colonies of up to 20 plants.

Historically, there were 3 or 4 sites for this species in the central New York area; the only extant site is a disjunct population, with the nearest known occurrence being hundreds of miles away in Ontario. It is more common in the western mountains and northward in Canada.

Our most attractive coralroot, its brilliantly colored candy-striped flowers light up the dark forest habitat that it frequents.

Other Names: Hooded Coralroot, Macrae's Coralroot, Striped Coral-root.

Name Origin: Derived from the Latin word *striatus*—"striped"—referring to the purplish stripes on the floral parts.

Identification: 4 to 20 inches (10–60 cm) tall.

Only other coralroots could be confused with this species. It is easily distinguished when blooming from the other species by its striking red-striped flowers. When in bud or in fruit, it is hard to differentiate from spotted coralroot. Albino forms lacking the purple pigment sometimes occur. Parasitic wasps are reported as pollinators. Vegetative reproduction via

spreading rhizomes is common; self-fertilization also occurs.

Abundance: Very rare in NE & NY, with one known extant site near Syracuse, NY.

Range: British Columbia east to Newfoundland, south to California and south through the Rocky Mountains to west Texas, Minnesota, Wisconsin, Michigan and New York. Also found in Mexico.

Nature Notes:

The lip, when struck by sunlight, has been likened to the "glowing color of a fine ruby."

The flowers droop down and are best viewed from ground level.

Early Coralroot
Corallorhiza trifida

| APRIL | MAY | JUNE | JULY | AUG | SEPT | OCT |

Rich or moist forests.

Nature Notes:

The stems, flowers and seed capsules of this species contain trace amounts of chlorophyll; hence the plant may not be totally dependent on the associated mycorrhizal fungi for nutrition.

The bright green seed capsules are easier to spot than the diminutive blooming plants, and are much larger.

In the northern portion of the range, plants are often suffused with bronze and the floral parts with purple spots (inset photo above.)

An early spring ephemeral that is the "greenest" of our coralroots, with trace amounts of chlorophyll.

Other Names: Northern Coralroot, Yellow Coralroot, Pale Coralroot, Three-parted Coralroot, Spring Coralroot, Early Coral-root.

Name Origin: The name, *trifida*, is from the Latin *trifidus*, "cleft into three parts," referring to the three-lobed lip of the species.

Identification: 3 to 14 inches (8–35 cm) tall.

This species can be distinguished from other coralroots by its earlier blooming time, small stature, tiny greenish-white flowers and distinctive seed capsules. It can be confused with the yellow form of Spotted Coralroot.

A bronze specimen

developing seed capsules

seed capsules

Abundance: Found throughout NE & NY; more common northward.

Range: Circumboreal; Alaska east to Newfoundland, south in the mountains to California, Arizona and New Mexico, Minnesota east to Maine and south to West Virginia; Europe and northern Asia.

Nature Notes:

Although chiefly self-pollinated, syrphid flies sometimes play a role in their pollination.

Pink Lady's-slipper (Moccasin Flower)
Cypripedium acaule

pouch color variations

| APRIL | MAY | JUNE | JULY | AUG | SEPT | OCT |

Mixed hardwood and coniferous forests; dry, acidic soils.

Nature Notes:

The lip is usually pink but all shades occur from pure white to an intense magenta with dark crimson veins. The white-flowered forma *albiflorum* (photo above) is more frequent northward in NE, whereas the two-flowered forma *biflorum* and the narrow-leaved forma *lancifolium* are both rare.

The opening to the pouch is different from all other species of the genus in North America; instead of being round, it is a longitudinal slit running down the length of the sac.

One of the most frequently encountered orchids in eastern North America.

Other Names: Pink Moccasin-flower, Stemless Lady's-slipper, Two-leaved Lady's-slipper, Noah's Ark, Squirrel-shoes, Camel's-foot, Stemless Lady's-slipper.

Name Origin: *acaule*, from the Greek *a*, meaning "without" and the Latin *caulis*, meaning "stalk or stem" referring to the fact that there is no above-ground stem; the true stem is underground.

Identification: 4 to 16 inches (10–40 cm) tall.

The basal pair of large, deeply ribbed, and hairy leaves and the pink pouch with longitudinal aperture easily distinguishes this species from all other lady's-slippers.

seed capsule

The defining characteristic of the genus is the lip petal, which has evolved into a distinctive and very attractive pouch-shaped "slipper." And it is an important structure in pollination (see pg. 2).

Abundance: Occasional to frequent throughout our area.

Range: Northwest Territories east to Newfoundland, south through Minnesota to Alabama and Georgia.

Nature Notes:

Favors dry soils but also grows in sphagnum bogs and fens.

As one proceeds northward, it becomes one of the rarer species of the genus.

Ram's-head Lady's-slipper
Cypripedium arietinum

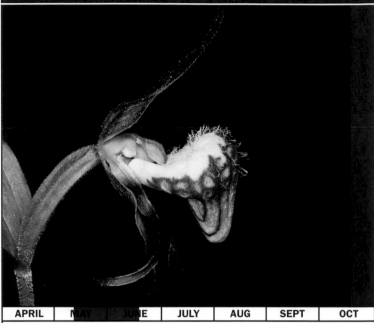

| APRIL | MAY | JUNE | JULY | AUG | SEPT | OCT |

Two distinct habitats: in N White Cedar swamps, in wet sphagnum; and in thin, dry soils over limestone; always in at least partial shade.

Nature Notes:

This species is of conservation concern in every state and province it occurs.

In Vermont, Ram's-head Lady's-slipper grows in base-rich, shallow soils on Lake Champlain headlands.

The flowers of Ram's-head Lady's-slipper have been reported to be ephemeral, but they usually remain in good condition until they are pollinated.

After pollination, the dorsal sepal reclines over the aperture, and the flower quickly senesces.

This species is the smallest and daintiest of the eastern lady's-slippers. The flowers are about the size of the tip of your finger.

Other Names: Ram's-head Orchid, Ram's-head, Ram's-head Cypripedium, Chandler's Cypripedium, Steeple-cap.

Name Origin: From the Latin *arientinus,* meaning "of a ram" (from *aries,* "a ram"), referring to the imagined resemblance of the flower to the head of a ram complete with horns.

Identification: 4 to 12 inches (10–30 cm) tall.

The flower shape is distinctive and easily distinguishes the species. It is our only lady's-slipper with lateral sepals that are not fused.

Abundance: Rare and local. Likely extirpated in Connecticut.

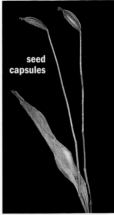

seed
capsules

In the rare forma *albiflorum*, the lip is whitish with pale green veining, and the petals and sepals are pale yellow-green.

Range: From Maine to Massachusetts west around the Great Lakes to Lake Winnipeg in Manitoba. In many parts of this range its distribution is very spotty.

Small White Lady's-slipper
Cypripedium candidum

APRIL	MAY	JUNE	JULY	AUG	SEPT	OCT

Calcareous fens, in full sunlight.

Nature Notes:

Historically, *C. candidum* was primarily a prairie species. The center of its original range was in the northeastern Great Plains where millions and millions of Small White Lady's-slippers co-existed with Bison.

Because *C. candidum* is shade-intolerant, it declines at sites where shrubs and trees invade.

One of the most imperiled of all lady's-slippers in North America.

Other Names: White Lady's-slipper, Silver Slipper, Violet-veined White Slipper, Moccasin-flower, White Frauenschuh.

Name Origin: From the Latin *candidus*, meaning "shining white" referring to the lip.

Identification: 2 to 2 inches (2–2 cm) tall.

This lady's-slipper, with its shining white flowers, cannot be mistaken for any other orchid species.

The flowers have a delicate fragrance that can be detected from as far away as a meter.

In early spring, the flowers open usually before the leaves unwrap from around the stem.

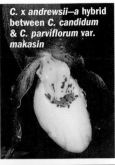

C. x *andrewsii*—a hybrid between *C. candidum* & *C. parviflorum* var. *makasin*

seed capsule

The white lip is often spotted with purple around the opening and streaked with purple within; at the back of the lip, the outer veins are various shades of purple.

Abundance: Very rare, only a few remnant populations extant in the vicinity of Rochester, NY; the largest population is in Bergen Swamp. Historically and currently absent from New England.

Range: Saskatchewan south to Nebraska, east to western New York, south to Missouri, Kentucky, and New Jersey; Alabama.

Nature Notes:

Cypripedium x *andrewsii* is the hybrid between *C. candidum* and *C. parviflorum* var. *makasin* (photo above).

Small Northern Yellow Lady's-slipper
Cypripedium parviflorum var. makasin

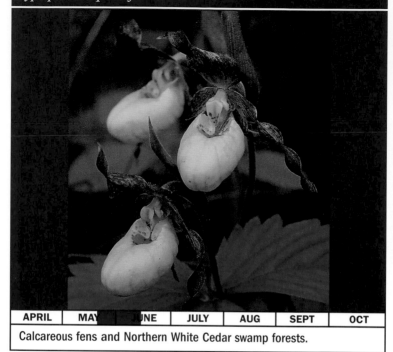

APRIL	MAY	JUNE	JULY	AUG	SEPT	OCT

Calcareous fens and Northern White Cedar swamp forests.

Nature Notes:

Variety *makasin* is the more common of the two small-flowered yellow lady's-slippers in NE & NY and can be found in scattered populations. The plants, with their rich yellow flowers with scarlet to purple markings within the lip, are a joy to behold when discovered in a remote fen.

Pollinators are likely small bees; it also reproduces vegetatively along spreading rhizomes.

An intensely sweet-smelling and diminutive lady's-slipper with attractive mahogany-red or dark brown sepals and petals.

Other Names: Lesser Yellow Lady's-slipper, Northern Small Yellow Lady's-slipper.

Name Origin: The varietal name, *makasin*, is the Algonquin name for the shoe-shaped flowers.

Identification: 5 to 20 inches (10–60 cm) tall.

The differentiating characteristics of variety *makasin* are: a smooth or inconspicuously pubescent upper sheathing bract at the base of the stem; the reddish-brown or red-purple color of the lateral petals being due to an even suffusion of pigment; an intensely sweet floral scent; and its high-pH fen or lake shore habitat.

Abundance: Locally scattered in NE & NY in calcareous wetlands; usually in small populations.

Range: British Columbia south to Washington and Idaho, eastward from Alberta to Newfoundland, south to Illinois, Pennsylvania and New Jersey. More frequent in Canada.

Map Note: Because most herbarium records in New England and New York have yet to be updated in regards to the recently named varieties of *C. parviflorum*, only one map for that species is provided, without regard to variety (see *C. p.* var. *pubescens* on pg 59). Further range information is given within each varietal description.

Nature Notes:

One or two ribbed seed capsules, often with dried flower remnants, persist all winter. It is a species of regional conservation concern.

Very rare anthocyanin-free electric-green form, a mutation lacking any red pigment.

Small Southern Yellow Lady's-slipper
Cypripedium parviflorum var. parviflorum

APRIL	MAY	JUNE	JULY	AUG	SEPT	OCT

Dry to moist deciduous forest, favors acidic soils.

Nature Notes:

This is the rarest of the three varieties of yellow lady's-slippers in NE & NY. Many historical populations no longer exist. The flowers, though tiny, are intensely beautiful. Pollinators are likely small bees; it also reproduces vegetatively along spreading rhizomes. One or two ribbed seed capsules, often with dried flower remnants, persist all winter. It is a species of regional conservation concern.

A small-flowered and uncommon yellow lady's-slipper with a pleasant rose-like fragrance.

Other Names: None.

Name Origin: The varietal name, *parviflorum*, means "small flowered."

Identification: 5 to 20 inches (10–60 cm) tall.

The differentiating characteristics of variety *parviflorum* are: a conspicuously pubescent upper sheathing bract at the base of the stem; its red-purple colored lateral petals comprised of densely spaced dots; a rose-like or musty floral scent; and its dry, low-pH, deciduous woods habitat.

Abundance: Rare and local in NE & NY. It can be found in the Southern Tier and mid-Hudson Valley areas of NY and sporadically eastward into CT, MA, RI, VT.

Range: Kansas east to Massachusetts, south to Arkansas and Georgia. It is most abundant in the southern prairie states.

Map Note: Because most herbarium records in New England and New York have yet to be updated in regards to the recently named varieties of *C. parviflorum*, only one map for that species is provided (see page 59).

Large Yellow Lady's-slipper
Cypripedium parviflorum var. pubescens

APRIL	MAY	JUNE	JULY	AUG	SEPT	OCT

Found in various habitats, including rich woodlands to bogs, swamps and fens, more common in alkaline areas.

Nature Notes:

One of the most attractive of our native orchids and much sought after by gardeners because it can be cultivated. Plants should never be dug from the wild! Variety pubescens is pollinated by andrenid and halictid bees. One or two ribbed seed capsules, often with dried flower remnants, persist all winter. It is a species of regional conservation concern.

The largest and most common of our yellow lady's-slippers; one of the choicest species of the springtime floral pageant in our region.

Other Names: Greater Yellow Lady's-slipper, Yellow Lady's-slipper, Common Yellow Lady's-slipper.

Name Origin: The varietal name, *pubescens*, means "downy" in Latin in reference to the hairs that cover the stems and leaves.

Identification: 7 to 30 inches (18–75 cm) tall.

Variety *pubescens* has been frequently misidentified in NE & NY. The major differentiating characteristic of variety *pubescens* is the larger lip, which ranges from 1 to 2 ½ inches (4–6 cm) long. Also, varieties *parviflorum* and *makasin* have a stronger floral fragrance than pubescens, which is faint and musky. It was

seed
capsule

long believed that it occurred exclusively in deciduous forests and this is the case in southern NE & NY. In northern NE it also occurs in N. White Cedar (*Thuja occidentalis*) swamps and in these populations the plants have smooth sheathing bracts, a distinct departure from the usual densely pubescent sheathing bracts that have been used to identify the variety. The sepals and petals are similarly colored and highly variable; ranging from yellowish-green with brown or reddish veining to pure green or pure yellow or rarely dark brown. Populations with dark brown sepals and petals—a floral trait associated with the other two varieties—further adds to difficulty in identification.

Abundance: Locally scattered in NE & NY in neutral to calcareous woodlands and fens, more frequent northward.

Range: Very widespread across most of the continent from Alaska east to Newfoundland, absent from the central and southern prairies and arid regions of the west, where it is rare at higher elevations in the Rockies south to Arizona and New Mexico; south to northern Georgia in the east.

Showy Lady's-slipper
Cypripedium reginae

| APRIL | MAY | JUNE | JULY | AUG | SEPT | OCT |

Calcareous fens, swamps, moist meadows and woods.

Nature Notes:

The largest and showiest of the lady's-slippers in NE & NY, there is no grander sight in all of nature than a fen lit up by the myriad peppermint-colored blossoms of this unforgettable species, whose populations can often number in the thousands with groups of many dozen stems.

One should plan on being up to your knees (or deeper!) in saturated muck, the principal substrate of the species. Seepage of groundwater is essential and keeps the soil cool and moist, thereby allowing this northern plant to survive at more southern latitudes.

A tall, regal, lady's-slipper with stunning red and white blossoms; one of the undisputed orchid-prizes of our region.

Other Names: Showy Lady's-slipper, Queen Lady's-slipper, Pink-and-white Lady's-slipper.

Name Origin: The Latin word *reginae* means "queen" and refers to the regal qualities of this stunning orchid.

Identification: 8 to 36 inches (20–91 cm) tall.

With its large, regal stature and showy pink and white flowers, this species stands apart from all other *Cypripediums*.

Abundance: Infrequent but locally common in NE & NY. It is a species of regional conservation concern.

rare white form

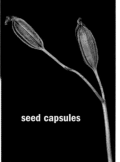

seed capsules

It is still abundant in many parts of its range, in spite of the plant-plunderers that have threatened its existence.

Several populations have been exterminated by digging or, unbelievably, over-zealous botanists collecting specimens for herbaria. Fortunately, mega-populations of up to 10,000 plants still occur in some swamps.

Range: Saskatchewan east to Newfoundland, south to Arkansas and northern North Carolina.

Nature Notes:

The plants are slow-growing and require at least 15 years before reaching blooming size.

Pollinators are bees, but it also reproduces vegetatively along spreading rhizomes.

Broad-leaved Helleborine
Epipactis helleborine

| APRIL | MAY | JUNE | JULY | AUG | SEPT | OCT |

Many habitats; mesic forests, roadsides, and disturbed soils, even in urban settings. Occurs in native habitats where it acts like a native species.

Nature Notes:

Concoctions from the roots and rhizomes have been used as remedies for various ills, including gout.

The outer, heart-shaped segment of the lip protrudes and curves under, thus offering a landing place for pollinators.

The species seems indifferent to soil conditions and habitat, it even colonizes garbage dumps.

This non-native species was first found in North America near Syracuse, NY, in 1879, and has migrated across the continent all the way to the Pacific Coast.

Other Names: Common Helleborine, Eastern Helleborine, Bastard Hellebore, Helleborine Orchid, Helleborine.

Name Origin: *helleborine* means "like a helle-bore"

Identification: 4 to 32 inches (10–80 cm) tall.

No similar species, although the leaves may superficially resemble some species of *Cypripedium*. The variation in flower color includes shades and mixtures of green, yellow, and purple.

seed
capsules

Abundance: Common.

Range: Eastern North America; southeastern California; scattered in western North America; Eurasia.

Nature Notes:

The common wasp, *Vespula vulgaris*, is reported to be the sole pollinator in New England; in Europe the pollinator is another wasp, *Vespa sylvestris*.

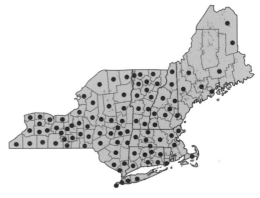

Showy Orchid
Galearis spectabilis

APRIL	MAY	JUNE	JULY	AUG	SEPT	OCT

Rich mesic or calcareous woodlands, often on slopes and streamsides. In NE, it also occurs in Hemlock forests.

Nature Notes:

Some botanists report that Showy Orchis responds favorably to disturbance, even colonizing early successional habitats, but others restrict the plant to climax, unspoiled forests.

Showy Orchis is in prime flower when the forest leaves have expanded to about three-fourths full size. Its frequent companions are trillium, spring beauty, and hepatica.

Showy Orchis often grows in moist spots not far from temporary spring ponds.

One of our most cherished spring wildflowers.

Other Names: Purple-hooded Orchis, Purple Orchis, Mauve-hood Orchis, Gay Orchis, Two-leaved Orchis, Kirtle-pink, Showy Orchis.

Name Origin: From the Latin *spectabilis* meaning "remarkable or showy" in reference to the showy flowers.

Identification: 4 to 12 inches (10–30 cm) tall.

The shape and color of the flower is unlike any other orchid in our region. Sterile plants of Showy Orchis are sometimes difficult to distinguish from sterile plants of Lily-leaved Twayblade. The fleshy, almost succulent, glossy green leaves of Showy Orchis are distinctive.

There are two described forms of Showy Orchis from our region: forma *gordinierii* has

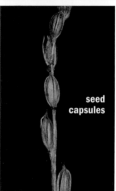

seed
capsules

white flowers and forma *willeyi* has pinkish-purple flowers. Sometimes, in pure *G. spectabilis* plants, the purple of the sepals and petals spills over onto the lip, where all combinations of color mixture occur. Sometimes the entire flower is a rich red-lilac color and other times it is faint pink, or the pigment is concentrated on the lip as stripes or indistinct spots.

Abundance: Occasional to frequent in NY and VT; local in CT and MA; rare in NH, ME, and RI.

Range: Occurs throughout most of the northeastern quarter of the United States south through the mid-Atlantic states. In NE & NY, it is absent only from northern Maine.

Giant Rattlesnake Plantain
Goodyera oblongifolia

APRIL	MAY	JUNE	JULY	AUG	SEPT	OCT

Dry conifer, hardwood, or mixed forest.

Nature Notes:

In rare cases, the leaves are marked with handsome reticulations (forma *reticulata*). The pollinators are unconfirmed but are probably small bees. The plants also spread prolifically via spreading rhizomes and often form large colonies.

The largest of the *Goodyera*, it is an uncommon species in our region.

Other Names: Western Rattlesnake-Plantain, Menzies's Rattlesnake-Plantain, Green-leaved Rattlesnake-Plantain, Giant Rattlesnake Orchis.

Name Origin: The name is derived from two Latin words: *oblongus*, "oblong" and *folium* "leaf," referring to the egg-shaped leaves.

Identification: 8 to 20 inches (15–50 cm) tall.

This species is easily distinguished from other *Goodyera* species by its unique leaves with a distinctive white stripe along the center, by the larger pear-shaped flowers with coppery-green overlays (the flowers of the other three *Goodyera* species are more spherical in shape) on a one-sided spike, by larger leaves, and greater height.

seed
capsules

Abundance: Very rare and local in Aroostook County, Maine; one record from northern Vermont.

Range: Southeastern Alaska to Newfoundland, south to Maine, California and New Mexico; Mexico. It is most common in the western mountains.

Downy Rattlesnake Plantain
Goodyera pubescens

APRIL	MAY	JUNE	JULY	AUG	SEPT	OCT

Mixed and deciduous woods.

Nature Notes:

Goodyera pubescens is a southern species reaching the northern limit of its range in NE & NY.

In the southern portion of NE & NY it is one of the most frequently encountered orchid species.

It has the most handsomely marked foliage of any of our native orchids which has led to the very destructive inclusion of the species in mail order terrarium kits, causing serious population declines (or extirpation) in some areas.

The attractively reticulated, evergreen leaves of this orchid are a visual treat in any season.

Other Names: Downy Rattlesnake Orchis, Adder's Violet, Net-leaf, Spotted Plantain, Rattlesnake Leaf, Scrofula-weed.

Name Origin: The Latin word *pubescens* means "growing hair" or "downy," referring to the densely pubescent inflorescence.

Identification: 9 to 20 inches (20–50 cm) tall.

Goodyera pubescens is the showiest of the *Goodyera* species in NE & NY. Its basal rosette of attractively reticulated leaves and snow-white, pubescent blossoms on a many-flowered spike set it apart from the other members of the genus.

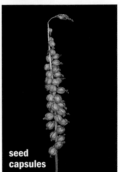

seed
capsules

Abundance: Widespread and common in the southern portion of NE & NY, becoming rare northward.

Range: From Nova Scotia and central Maine south to northern Georgia, west to the Mississippi River and the western edge of the Great Lakes to southern Ontario.

Nature Notes:

Tiny "mining bees" (*Augochlorella striata*) have been documented as pollinators.

Lesser Rattlesnake Plantain
Goodyera repens

APRIL	MAY	JUNE	JULY	AUG	SEPT	OCT

Moist coniferous forests. A very shallow rooted species, it usually grows on moss to utilize the higher moisture content

Nature Notes:

When it first blooms, the flower opens only enough to allow the pollinator to touch the pollinia; after the initial removal of pollen the lip descends enough to allow the next visitor to deposit pollen on the now receptive stigma. Moths, butterflies and bumblebees have been documented as pollinators. The plants also spread prolifically via spreading rhizomes and often form large colonies.

Goodyera repens is the smallest of the rattlesnake orchids.

The smallest of the *Goodyera*, this species is noted for its strikingly marked leaves; it is easiest to locate when blooming.

Other Names: Dwarf Rattlesnake Plantain, Creeping Rattlesnake Plantain.

Name Origin: The Latin word *repens* means "creeping" in reference to its method of propagation by underground rhizomes.

Identification: 2 to 2 inches (2–2 cm) tall.

Compared to the similar *G. tesselata*, this species has smaller leaves that are darker green with wider and bolder white markings (*forma ophioides*) or in the case of the nominate variety repens, pure green leaves with no markings. It tends to have fewer and smaller flowers on a one-sided spike. The lip is narrower and is deeply concave with a proportionally longer

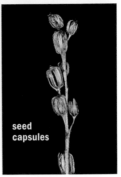

seed
capsules

tip that has been likened to the curving spout
of a teapot. It is easily differentiated from the
similarly reticulated *G. pubescens* by its much
smaller size and one-sided flower spike.

Abundance: Rare and local southward in NE
& NY; more widespread in northern coniferous forests.

Range: A circumboreal species, occurring
from Alaska east to Newfoundland and south
to the mountains of Tennessee in the east
and New Mexico in the west. It also
inhabits a wide band stretching
from Japan to northern
Britain.

Nature Notes:

G. repens was one of the
species featured by
Charles Darwin in his two
books on orchid pollina-
tion (1884 and 1887).

Checkered Rattlesnake Plantain
Goodyera tesselata

APRIL	MAY	JUNE	JULY	AUG	SEPT	OCT

Mixed and deciduous woodlands.

Nature Notes:

Goodyera tesselata is believed to be of hybrid origin, resulting from an ancient cross between *G. repens* and *G. oblongifolia*. This hybrid has extended its range much further than one of its parents; *G. tesselata* occurs occasionally in much of NE & NY, but *G. oblongifolia* occurs only at a few locations in far northern Maine, and historically from Vermont.

This *Goodyera* species is characterized by less colorful, checkered leaves; the tea pot-shaped flowers are very interesting when magnified.

Other Names: Checkered Rattlesnake Orchis, Tesselated Rattlesnake-Plantain, Loddiges's Rattlesnake-Plantain.

Name Origin: The Latin word *tesselatus* means "checkered" referring to the markings on the leaves.

Identification: 5 to 14 inches (15–35 cm) tall.

Compared to the similar *G. repens*, this species has larger leaves that are a lighter bluish-green with a more delicate and fainter pattern of markings. It tends to have more numerous and larger flowers that are randomly arranged on the spike. The lip is wider with a shorter tip

seed
capsules

that has been compared to the curving spout of a teapot. It is easily differentiated from *G. pubescens* by its much duller and only faintly reticulated leaves.

Abundance: Occasional to frequent in northern NE & NY; infrequent and local in southern NE & NY.

Range: Manitoba east to Newfoundland, south to Minnesota and Virginia.

Small Whorled Pogonia
Isotria medeoloides

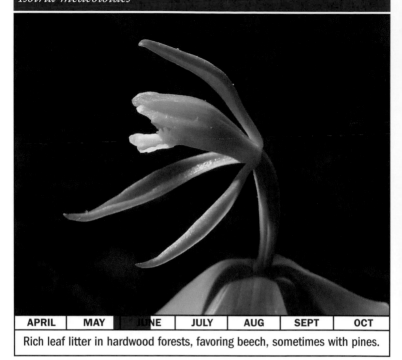

APRIL	MAY	JUNE	JULY	AUG	SEPT	OCT

Rich leaf litter in hardwood forests, favoring beech, sometimes with pines.

Nature Notes:

In late May 2010, Small Whorled Pogonia was found in Orange County, New York, after not being seen in that state for more than 30 years even though botanists had been diligently searching for it.

Small Whorled Pogonia may have extended periods of underground dormancy, lasting up to 20 years.

Small Whorled Pogonia does not form extensive clumps vegetatively, as does the Large Whorled Pogonia; rather, widely scattered plants are the rule.

Often considered to be the rarest orchid east of the Mississippi River and north of Florida. This species was one of the first orchids listed by the federal government under the Endangered Species Act.

Other Names: Lesser Whorled Pogonia, Smaller Whorled Pogonia Orchid, Small Whorled Crest-lip, Green Five-leaved Orchid.

Name Origin: Named for the genus *Medeola* and *–oides* meaning "resembling" because of the similarity of the leaves of the two plants. *Medeola* is named for the mythological Greek goddess *Medea*.

Identification: 3 to 10 inches (8–25 cm) tall.

The flower shape is distinctive and easily distinguishes the species. See genus description for identification of sterile plants.

Don't be confused by the whorl of leaves of the Indian Cucumber-Root (*Medeola virginiana*) which do resemble those of *I. medeoloides*.

Abundance: Rare to local throughout NE and NY. Probably extirpated in VT where it has not been seen for nearly 100 years.

No more than three or four plants usually occur in a population, but in NH and western ME the Small Whorled Pogonia can be locally abundant, totaling several thousand plants in both states.

Range: Michigan east to Maine, south to Missouri and South Carolina.

Nature Notes:

Frederick Pursh first described this species in 1814, and since then it has been seen only infrequently.

Plants with two flowers are an uncommon find.

Large Whorled Pogonia
Isotria verticillata

APRIL	MAY	JUNE	JULY	AUG	SEPT	OCT

Mesic, acidic deciduous forests.

Nature Notes:

Large Whorled Pogonia frequently forms extensive clones with hundreds of stems.

Large Whorled Pogonia is pollinated by solitary bees and is apparently self-compatible.

Flowers of the Large Whorled Pogonia seldom last more than 3 to 4 days in good condition.

The long, slender, spreading sepals give this orchid a bizarre appearance that radically differs from all other native orchids in our region.

Other Names: Whorled Pogonia, Five-leaved Orchid, Green Adderling, Large Whorled Crest-lip, Purple Five-leaved Orchid, Whorl-crest.

Name Origin: The name *verticillata* is a Latin adjective meaning "whorled" referring to the whorl of leaves at the top of the stem.

Identification: 5 to 12 inches (13–30 cm) tall.

The size and shape of the spectacular sepals are unmistakable. See genus description for identification of sterile plants.

The blossom is a remarkable sight. The 2-inch sepals are drawn back with the straggling effect of wavy ribbons—or perhaps sprawling spider

seed capsule

A rare shot of a Pink Lady's-slipper next to a Large Whorled Pogonia.

legs. The corolla is thrust forward in the shape of a funnel, its upper half formed by the pair of over-arching petals. The white lip is flanked on each side with dull purple streaks. The overall effect is of some kind of strange insect waiting to pounce.

Abundance: Locally common in southern NE & NY, rare to local in northern NE & NY.

Range: Michigan east to southern Maine, south to Texas and Florida.

Lily-leaved Twayblade
Liparis liliifolia

| APRIL | MAY | JUNE | JULY | AUG | SEPT | OCT |

Rich, mesic forests and streamsides, often in calcareous soils.

Nature Notes:

In contrast to its rarity in the Northeast, Lily-leaved Twayblade is one of the more common woodland orchids in the Midwest.

Human activities such as habitat destruction are largely responsible for the rapid decline of Lily-leaved Twayblade in NE & NY.

The green-flowered forma *viridiflora* is a very rare find in our region.

Populations in our region have dramatically crashed during the past 60 years, making this orchid a rare find in the Northeast.

Other Names: Large Twayblade, Mauve Sleekwort, Brown Wide-lip Orchid, Purple Scutcheon.

Name Origin: From the Latin *lilium*, "a lily," and *–folius*, "leaved" (from *folium*, "leaf"), hence lily-leaved, referring to the lily-like appearance of the leaves.

Identification: 4 to 10 inches (10–25 cm) tall.

Lily-leaved Twayblade can be distinguished from Loesel's Twayblade by examining the lips: those of the former are pale purple and about 10 mm long whereas the latter are yellowish-green and about 5 mm long.

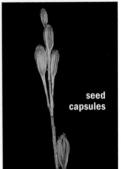

seed capsules

Abundance: Rare in NY and probably extirpated in the southeastern part of the state including all of Long Island; local in CT, MA, RI, VT; historical reports from ME and NH are based on misidentifications of *L. loeselii*.

Range: Minnesota and Ontario east to Massachusetts, south to Oklahoma and Georgia.

Loesel's Twayblade
Liparis loeselii

APRIL	MAY	JUNE	JULY	AUG	SEPT	OCT

Rich fens, calcareous peaty swamps, and mucky seepages. Open and forested habitats in permanently saturated soils.

Nature Notes:

The seed capsules are large for the size of the plant and often persist all winter.

It often grows in mucky or peaty soils and perhaps does best where the adjacent herbaceous vegetation is sparse.

Often overlooked due to its uniform yellow-green color and small size.

Other Names: Yellow Wide-lip Orchid, Fen Orchis, Bog Twayblade, Green Twayblade, Fen Orchid, Olive Scutcheon, Russet-witch.

Name Origin: Named by Linnaeus in honor of Johann Loesel, a 17th century German botanist and author of a Prussian flora

Identification: 2 to 10 inches (5–25 cm) tall.

Loesel's Twayblade can be distinguished from Lily-leaved Twayblade by examining the lips: those of the former are yellowish-green and about 5 mm long whereas the latter are pale purple and about 10 mm long. The leaves of *L. loeselii* are generally narrower, shorter, and yellower than those of *L. liliifolia*.

seed
capsules

Abundance: Occasional throughout.

Range: British Columbia east to Nova Scotia and southwestern Newfoundland, south to Arkansas and Mississippi and in the southern Appalachian Mountains; Europe.

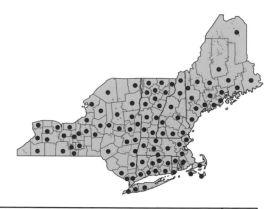

Auricled Twayblade
Listera auriculata

APRIL	MAY	JUNE	JULY	AUG	SEPT	OCT

Alder thickets, rocky riverbanks, and gravel bars.

Nature Notes:

One of the rarest orchids in North America, *Listera auriculata* has a very limited distribution in the upper Great Lakes, Atlantic Canada and NE & NY and is always a lucky find.

The diminutive plants prefer the rocky gravels of lakeshores and riverbanks, where the land is flooded and fresh soil is deposited by the water. They often grow under the cover of alders.

Due to the watery-green color of the blossoms the plants are easily overlooked, even though the leaves and flowers are much larger than both *L. australis* and *L. cordata*.

An elusive orchid whose favored habitat of streamside alder thickets makes for challenging photographic conditions; sitting in the river usually works best!

Other Names: None.

Name Origin: The name, *auriculata*, is from the Latin word *auricula*, "external ear" referring to the ear-like extension of the base of the lip around the column.

Identification: 2 to 10 inches (5–25 cm) tall.

The two-leaved *Listera* are easily differentiated from the one-leaved *Malaxis* —the other 'little green orchids'. The *Listera* species of NE & NY are easily differentiated from each other by lip shape (see page 20). The flower of *L. auriculata* is fascinating when magnified. The sepals and petals curve back to expose the lip, which

is oblong and somewhat constricted near the center and is divided into two oblong lobes near the tip; the auricles at the base of the lip turn inward and grasp the column. Up the center of the lip runs a dark-green groove leading to a minute recess containing nectar to coax the pollinator under the column which will then be triggered, depositing the pollinia.

Abundance: Rare and local, several sites are historical.

Recently discovered populations on the banks of the Hudson River in New York's Adirondack Mountains may represent the southern limit of this orchid's range.

Range: Ontario east to Newfoundland, south to the northern portions of Minnesota, Wisconsin, Michigan and New York, east to Maine.

Nature Notes:

A hybrid between *L. auriculata* and *L convallarioides* (*L. x veltmanii*) is often present when the two species grow together. Pollination is by unknown flying insects.

Southern Twayblade
Listera australis

APRIL	MAY	JUNE	JULY	AUG	SEPT	OCT

Open, wet woodlands in the southern portion of the range, cool sphagnum bogs in the north.

Nature Notes:

Listera australis is very rarely observed, due to its small stature, inconspicuous nature and inaccessible habitat preference. Individual flower size is 6–10 mm; a hand lens is recommended to appreciate it fully.

Considered by many orchid lovers to be the most attractive of the *Listera* species, it has been said that no garnet or ruby can surpass the crimson glow of its back-lighted blossoms. Like the Striped Coralroot, the color of the blossoms is greatly enhanced when illuminated by the sun.

A rare and easily overlooked gem of bogs and wetlands.

Other Names: Apiculate Cleft-lip, Shining Twayblade.

Name Origin: The name, *australis*, is Latin for "southern."

Identification: Up to 8 inches (20 cm) tall.

All *Listera* have two leaves, as opposed to the genus *Malaxis*—the other 'little green orchids'—which have one. The *Listera* species of NE & NY are easily differentiated from each other by lip shape (see page 20). The distinguishing characteristic of *L. australis* is the lip, which is linear and is split into two slender filaments. The flower color ranges from purple to pure green (*forma virescens*).

Abundance: Rare and local in NY; exceptionally rare in NE.

Range: Quebec to Nova Scotia, south to Florida and Texas.

Nature Notes:

The species sets seed very quickly; a month after flowering there is usually no sign of the plants until next season.

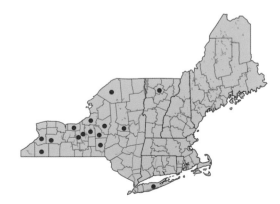

Broad-lipped Twayblade
Listera convallarioides

APRIL	MAY	JUNE	JULY	AUG	SEPT	OCT

Low moist rich woods and river banks.

Nature Notes:

Listera convallarioides is the largest of the twayblades in NE & NY and it often forms large colonies in damp woods and mossy glades and along stream banks.

A hybrid between L. auriculata and L convallarioides (L. x veltmanii) is often present when the two species grow together.

A short-lived plant, pollination is by unknown flying insects (probably fungus gnats as in other members of this genus).

An uncommon find along shaded riverbanks; the prominent two-lobed lip gives the plant a unique appearance.

Other Names: Broad-leaved Twayblade.

Name Origin: This species is named for the lily-of-the-valley genus *Convallaria*, and—*oides* "like," referring to its vague resemblance to the genus.

Identification: 2 to 12 inches (5–30 cm) tall.

The genus *Malaxis*—*the* other 'little green orchids'— have only one leaf, all *Listera* species have two. The *Listera* species of NE & NY are easily differentiated from each other by lip shape (see page 20). The wedge-shaped lip, which is widened and two-lobed at the tip and narrow at the base, distinguishes *L. convallarioides* from other *Listera* species.

Abundance: Never common, in NE & NY it is found locally through most of Maine, New Hampshire, Vermont and northeastern New York.

Range: From Newfoundland and Nova Scotia south to Maine and then west to Ontario and Minnesota; skipping to southern British Columbia; south along the coast through Oregon to the mountains of California; southward through the Rockies to southern Utah, Colorado and extreme southern Arizona.

Heart-leaved Twayblade
Listera cordata var. *cordata*

APRIL	MAY	JUNE	JULY	AUG	SEPT	OCT

Mossy, damp, coniferous or mixed coniferous-hardwood forests, sphagnum bogs and evergreen swamps.

Nature Notes:

One of the earliest blooming spring orchids in NE & NY, *L. cordata* often grows in large colonies; the flower color ranges from ruby-red to pure green (forma *virescens*). A woodland floor covered with these tiny jewel-like orchids and illuminated with sunlight is a marvelous sight.

After fertilization the seed ripens very rapidly and it is not uncommon to find fresh-looking blooms and capsules from which the seed has already been dispersed.

Fungus gnats and other tiny insects attracted to its foul smell are the pollinators.

The diaphanous flowers of this miniature orchid are amongst the first to appear each spring.

Other Names: Heartleaf Twayblade.

Name Origin: The name, *cordata*, is from the Latin word *cordatus*, "heart-shaped," referring to the heart-shaped leaves of the species.

Identification: 2 to 13 inches (5–33 cm) tall.

The two-leaved Listera are easily differentiated from the one-leaved *Malaxis* —the other 'little green orchids'. The *Listera* species of NE & NY are easily differentiated from each other by lip shape (see page 20). The lip of the Heart-leaved Twayblade is distinctively cleft for at least half its length into two pointed lobes. The leaves are somewhat heart-shaped, but the leaves of *L. australis* are occasionally heart-

Paired leaves are half way up the stem but may appear lower when found in deep sphagnum moss.

ripening ovary

shaped as well, so leaf shape should not be a determining factor in identification. When in bloom the two species are easily differentiated.

Abundance: Present throughout NE & NY. This is the most frequently encountered *Listera* species in the northern portion of our region. Extirpated in Rhode Island.

Range: Circumboreal. From Great Britain through Europe, Asia to Alaska then east to Greenland, south to California, in the Rockies south to New Mexico, in the Appalachians south to North Carolina.

White Adder's-mouth
Malaxis monophyllos var. brachypoda

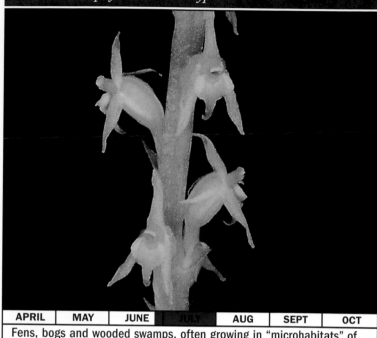

APRIL	MAY	JUNE	JULY	AUG	SEPT	OCT

Fens, bogs and wooded swamps, often growing in "microhabitats" of neutral reaction in acid conditions.

Nature Notes:

Was long considered a separate species (*M. brachypoda*) but most botanists now consider it to be a variety of the European species *M. monophyllos*. In the European variety the lip is uppermost, or non-resupinate. In the North American variety it is lowermost, or resupinate.

Fungus gnats have been suggested as pollinators.

The tiny plants are usually hidden in moss and bog vegetation and can easily be overlooked by even the most diligent orchid hunter.

The delicate flowers are some of the tiniest amongst orchids and are best appreciated under magnification.

Other Names: White Adder's-mouth Orchid.

Name Origin: From the Greek *monos*—"solitary," and *phyllon*—"leaf," referring to the single leaf; *brachys*—"short," and *podion*—"foot," referring to the short pedicel of the variety.

Identification: 4 to 10 inches (10–25 cm) tall.

Heart-Leaved Twayblade is the other orchid in our region with small greenish flowers, but has two leaves half-way up the stem. White Adder's-mouth has a single leaf, also half-way up the stem. Green Adder's-mouth is one-leaved as well, but the flowers are distinctly different in shape, color and arrangement along the raceme. Individual flower size is 1.5–3.0 mm.

Tiny orchids! For scale, compare to then 8-year-old Johanna's fingers.

Abundance: This is an uncommon orchid in NE & NY and is easily overlooked. Most populations are small, numbering a dozen plants or less.

Range: Southern Alaska east to Newfoundland, south to British Columbia, Minnesota east to Nova Scotia, south to Pennsylvania. There are disjunct populations in California and Colorado.

Green Adder's-mouth *Malaxis unifolia*
Bayard's Adder's-mouth *Malaxis bayardii*

| APRIL | MAY | JUNE | JULY | AUG | SEPT | OCT |

Acidic soils in woodlands, bogs, fens and meadows.

Nature Notes:

Bayard's Adder's-mouth (*Malaxis bayardii*) a globally threatened species, is very similar to *M. unifolia* in appearance. Historically found in eleven states in eastern North America, it is currently known from less than ten extant sites. As with many species of *Malaxis*, it may not be rare, but simply be overlooked.

The lip has two prominent lobes and with a little imagination, they can be seen as the fangs of a green, vegetative viper—"adder's mouth."

This interesting orchid is widespread but inconspicuous.

Other Names: Green Adder's-mouth Orchid.

Name Origin: The name, *unifolia*, is derived from the Latin words *unus*—"one" and *folium*—"leaf" in reference to the solitary leaf.

Identification: 3 to 12 inches (8–30 cm) tall.

The distinctive raceme distinguishes this species from White Adder's-mouth. When viewed from above the developing raceme has a unique sunburst pattern that may aid in finding this elusive species.

The distinguishing characteristics of *M. bayardii* are: longer-lasting yellowish green flowers on shorter pedicels, with a more elongated spike instead of the crowded flat-topped spike of *M. unifolia*; more prominent lobes on

Malaxis bayardii

seed
capsules

the base of the lip and drier habitats such as oak and pine barrens.

Abundance: Occasional to local in NE & NY; often overlooked.

Range: Manitoba east to Newfoundland south to Texas and Florida; Mexico.

M. unifolia from above.

Malaxis bayardii

Malaxis unifolia

Northern Green Bog-Orchid *Platanthera aquilonis*
Green Bog-Orchid *Platanthera huronensis*

P. huronensis

APRIL	MAY	JUNE	JULY	AUG	SEPT	OCT

Highly variable, from open moist or wet areas to shaded woodlands. Often occurs in roadside ditches and seeps.

Nature Notes:

These two species are part of the *Platanthera hyperborea* complex, a bewildering group that has proven difficult for botanists to classify.

In 1999 Dr. Charles Sheviak described *P. aquilonis* as a new species.

P. hyperborea is now considered limited to Iceland, Greenland, and the Hudson Bay region.

P. aquilonis is primarily self-pollinating, bumble-bees and moths pollinate *P. huronensis*, which also self-pollinates.

Classified as *Platanthera hyperborea* for many years; only recently recognized as separate species, identification can be a challenge.

Other Names: Leafy Green Orchid, Tall Northern Bog-Orchid, Northern Bog Orchid, Lake Huron Green Orchid (*P. huronensis*).

Name Origin: The name, *aquilonis*, is Latin for "northern" in reference to its distribution within North America; *P. huronensis* was named for Lake Huron, where it was first collected.

Identification: *P. aquilonis*: 2 to 23 inches (5–60 cm) tall. *P. huronensis* can be much taller: 4 to 40 inches (10–100+ cm).

These two similar species have a different general appearance: *P. huronensis* is larger-flowered with whitish-green flowers, whereas the smaller-flowered *P. aquilonis* has a watery yellowish

P. aquilonis

P. huronensis

P. aquilonis

P. aquilonis

	flower	**lip**	**spur**	**smell**
P. aquilonis	yellowish-green lip drab yellow	lance-shaped straight sides	bluntly-clubbed 3/4 length of lip	odorless
P. huronensis	whitish-green lip whiter	lance-shaped bulging sides	tubular-shaped =length of lip	scented

or greenish-yellowish lip, with green sepals. The main technical difference between the two is the column (use a hand lens to view). In *P. huronensis* the anther sacs are oriented more vertically and are well-separated at the top. In *P. aquilonis* they are more horizontal and nearly touching. The pollinia (masses of waxy pollen) in *P. huronensis* are compact and maintained within the anther sacs. In *P. aquilonis* they fragment and commonly hang loose out of the sacs, or the pollen trails down into the stigma.

Abundance: *P. aquilonis* is rare to local; *P. huronensis* is scattered to occasional throughout. Both species are more frequent northward.

Range: Alaska east to Newfoundland, Maine, south to New Mexico and Iowa.

Combined range of *P. aquilonis* & *P. huronensis*.

Northern White Fringed Orchid
Platanthera blephariglottis var. blephariglottis

| APRIL | MAY | JUNE | JULY | AUG | SEPT | OCT |

Bogs, fens, seeps, open wet meadows, roadside ditches.

Nature Notes:

A rare hybrid with *P. cristata* is known as *P.* x *canbyi*.

Striking hybrids with *P. ciliaris* (*P.* x *bicolor*) can occur where the two species grow together (photo above).

In favorable conditions, thousands of plants blanket the landscape with snow white feathery plumes of flowers.

Other Names: White Fringed Orchis, White Fringed Orchid, Snowy Orchid, Plume-of-Navarre.

Name Origin: From the Greek *blepharon* meaning "eyelash" and *glotta*, meaning "tongue" referring to the tongue-shaped lip with finely fringed edges.

Identification: 10 to 24 inches (25–60 cm) tall.

A densely flowering stalk usually supports between 30 and 60 flowers.

The White Fringed Orchid closely resembles its cousin the Yellow Fringed Orchid and dried

Note the perfectly camouflaged crab spider tucked into the raceme, just waiting for its next unsuspecting victim.

herbarium collections are difficult to identify, but in fresh plants the flower color and other characteristics distinguish the two species.

Abundance: Widespread and local.

Range: Michigan east to Newfoundland, south to Georgia.

Nature Notes:

Plants with fringeless lips are rare and known as forma *holopetala*.

Pollinated by butterflies and moths, including small hawk-moths.

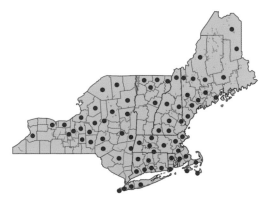

Yellow Fringed Orchid
Platanthera ciliaris

APRIL	MAY	JUNE	JULY	AUG	SEPT	OCT

Moist meadows, wet thickets, moist roadsides, lawns, and open sandy woods.

Nature Notes:

After one flowering season, a plant is usually able to send up only a few leaves the next season, as if to rest and gather strength for another year.

Hybrids of *P. ciliaris* with *P. blephariglottis* are *P. x bicolor* (see comments under *P. blephariglottis*).

One of our most striking native orchids.

The brilliant, deep yellow to orange flower plumes can tower three feet above ground level.

Other Names: Orange Fringed Orchis, Orange Fringed Orchid, Orange-plume, Rattlesnake's Master.

Name Origin: From the Latin *cilium* meaning "eyelid" or "eyelashes" referring to the finely fringed lip.

Identification: 10 to 40 inches (25–100 cm) tall.

Except for flower color, a near mirror-image of *P. blephariglottis* (see discussion under that species on page 96 for differences between the two species).

A Tiger Swallowtail, loaded with pollen visits *P. ciliaris*

Abundance: Rare and local; reports from NH and VT are suspect.

Range: Southern Michigan east to Massachusetts, south to Florida and Texas.

Hybrid between *P. ciliaris* and *P. blephariglottis* is called *P.* x *bicolor*.

Club-spur Orchid
Platanthera (Gymnadeniopsis) clavellata

White flowered
forma *slaughteri*

APRIL	MAY	JUNE	JULY	AUG	SEPT	OCT

Bogs, swampy woods, open seepy habitats with thin soil, wet roadsides and ditches; sometimes quite common in previously disturbed wet open habitats.

Nature Notes:

Plants with broader leaves and a smaller stature, described as var. *ophioglossoides*, are more common in the north and at higher elevations, but also occur throughout the range of the species; some populations display a complete range of leaf shape and plant height. Recent studies conclude that this variety is of no taxonomic significance.

Some botanists include this species in the genus *Gymnadeniopsis*. Since the early 1800s it has been placed in 7 different genera and orchid experts still do not agree on where it belongs.

The club-shaped spur readily distinguishes this delicate orchid when in flower.

Other Names: Green Wood-Orchid, Little Club-spur Orchid, Small Green Fringed-Orchid, Small Green Wood-Orchid, Woodland Orchid, Frog Spike, Green Rein Orchid.

Name Origin: From the Latin *clavellatus* meaning "club shaped" referring to the club-like thickening at the tip of the spur.

Identification: 4 to 14 inches (10–35 cm) tall.

This orchid has a single clasping leaf at its base and another about one-third the way up the stem. When in bud it superficially resembles adder's-tongue fern, *Ophioglossum.*

seed
capsules

In forma *slaughteri* the flowers are pure white; forma *wrightii* has spurless flowers.

Abundance: Occasional throughout.

Range: Newfoundland to Georgia, westward around the Great Lakes to eastern Texas.

Nature Notes:

Club-spur Orchid needs no pollinators because it is self-fertilizing.

Flower parts often persist for many weeks in good condition on the developing ovaries.

Orange Crested Orchid
Platanthera cristata

APRIL	MAY	JUNE	JULY	AUG	SEPT	OCT

Moist, sandy & peaty meadows, marshes, roadsides, & open pine woods.

Nature Notes:

Hybrids of *P. cristata* with *P. blephariglottis* are *P. x canbyi*, and with *P. ciliaris* are *P. x channelii*; forma *straminea* is a pale yellow-flowered form.

This showy orchid is at the extreme northern limit of its range in southeastern NY and MA.

Other Names: Crested Fringed Orchid, Crested Rein Orchid, Golden Fringe Orchid, Orange Crest, Crested Yellow Orchid.

Name Origin: From the Latin *cristatus* meaning "crested" referring to the crests on the petals.

Identification: 8 to 32 inches (20–80 cm) tall.

The short spur is a distinguishing characteristic when comparing *P. cristata* with its close look-alike, *P. ciliaris*; otherwise, the vegetative parts of the two species are very similar. The color of mature plants is usually a deeper orange than that of *P. ciliaris*, but a pale yellow color form occurs in isolated colonies.

forma *straminea*

Abundance: Very rare in Suffolk Co., NY, and
Bristol Co., MA. Reports from CT and RI are
incorrect.

Range: Southeastern Massachusetts south to
Florida and west to eastern Texas, primarily on
the coastal plain but also inland to Arkansas and
Tennessee.

White Bog Orchid (Bog Candles)
Platanthera dilatata var. dilatata

APRIL	MAY	JUNE	JULY	AUG	SEPT	OCT

Fens, seepages, peaty open wet habitats, swamps, wet roadside ditches.

Nature Notes:

Long Island, NY, is at the southeastern limit of this species range.

P. dilatata is the most common of the three bog orchid species in our range.

Floral parts do not wither immediately after pollination.

Hybrids between *P. dilatata* and *P. aquilonis/huronensis* do occur.

The tall and graceful, snowy white spires appear almost luminescent against the often drab background of its wetland habitat, inspiring the common name of bog candles.

Other Names: Bog Candles, Scentbottle, Bog Orchid, Boreal Bog-Orchid, Leafy White Orchis, Tall White Northern Orchid, Fragrant Orchid, Tall White Bog-Orchid.

Name Origin: From the Latin *dilatatus*, meaning "broadened" referring to the dilated base of the lip.

Identification: 10 to 40+ inches (25–100+ cm).

The flowers are white, whereas the other two similar bog-orchid species have green flowers. The broadly dilated lip is another distinguishing characteristic. The flowers have a strong spicy fragrance

seed capsules

Abundance: Occasional to frequent in northern NE & NY, rare to local in southern NE & NY. Rare or extirpated in CT.

Range: Alaska east to Newfoundland, south to California and New Mexico; Minnesota south to Indiana, Pennsylvania and New England.

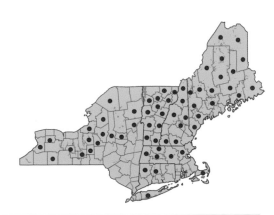

Northern Tubercled Orchid
Platanthera flava var. herbiola

APRIL	MAY	JUNE	JULY	AUG	SEPT	OCT

variable habitats, including open wet meadows, shaded floodplains, river shores, swamps, shrub thickets, roadside ditches and seeps.

Nature Notes:

The tubercle on the lip deflects the head and probing proboscis of a feeding insect into one of two pathways leading to a nectar-filled spur, often resulting in the attachment of the pollinium. Pollinators are mosquitoes and moths.

After pollination, the ovaries swell quickly and the petals and sepals often persist in fresh condition on the developing ovaries throughout much of the summer, thus extending the flowering season.

The prominent tubercle, or "bump," at the center of the base of the lip distinguishes this species.

Other Names: Pale-Green Orchid, Pale Green Orchis, Tubercled Rein-Orchid, Gypsy Spike.

Name Origin: *flava*: from the Latin *flavus* meaning "yellow" referring to the yellowish-green color of the flowers; *herbiola*: from the Latin *herbiola*, meaning "a little plant" possibly referring to the size of the type specimen.

Identification: 6 to 20 inches (15–50 cm) tall.

The lower two leaves are large and wide, the upper ones are abruptly narrower and bract-like. Sometimes confused with *Coeloglossum*

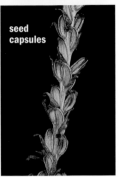

seed
capsules

viride var. *virescens*, but the prominent tubercle on the base of the lip is distinctive.

Abundance: Local to occasional throughout. Large colonies of 50 to 200 plants occur in our region, but often only a few individuals flower each season.

Range: Minnesota east to Nova Scotia, south to Missouri and western North Carolina.

Nature Notes:

A more southern variety, distinguished by darker colored flowers and significantly shorter flower bracts, does not enter our range.

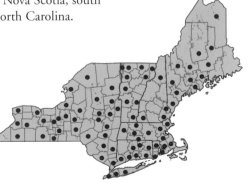

Large Purple Fringed Orchid
Platanthera grandiflora

| APRIL | MAY | JUNE | JULY | AUG | SEPT | OCT |

Wet areas; meadows, roadside ditches, seeps; open woodlands & swamps.

Nature Notes:

Frequently found along roadsides in wooded areas, leaving it vulnerable to road widening, mowing and winter salting of roads, as well as casual wildflower pickers.

It has been proposed that the differently shaped nectary openings attract different groups of pollinators. (See *P. psycodes* on pg. 124 for more info)

Tiger Swallowtail butterflies, small moths, and bumblebees have been documented pollinators.

A hybrid between *P. grandiflora* and *P. lacera* (*P. x keenani*) was described in 1994.

This tall, handsome orchid is one of the showcase species of NE & NY; its magnificent floral displays are a highlight of the summer season.

Other Names: Large Butterfly Orchid, Plume-royal, Greater Purple Fringed Orchid.

Name Origin: Derived from two Latin words: *grandis*, "large" and *floris*, "flower," meaning large-flowered.

Identification: 6 to 50 inches (15–100 cm) tall.

The flower color ranges from purple to white. The two purple fringed orchids that occur in NE & NY (*P. grandiflora*, *P. psycodes*) are similar in appearance and have long been a source of confusion and debate amongst botanists. Recent studies have codified some key differences between the two species: most importantly, the column of *P. psycodes* is relatively

Platanthera shriveri
Shriver's Frilly Orchid

narrow and the nectary opening is shaped like a transverse dumb-bell; in *P. grandiflora*, the column is much larger and the nectary opening is round. In addition, the flowers and oblong-shaped raceme of *P. grandiflora* are usually over twice as large as those of *P. psycodes*, which is characterized by a smaller-flowered, tapered raceme, but size alone is not a determining factor. Also, the flowers of *P. grandiflora* are more deeply-fringed than those of *P. psycodes*. In NE & NY, *P. grandiflora* blooms approximately two weeks earlier. There is also a white-flowered form (forma *albiflora*).

Abundance: Although less-common than its smaller, look-alike relation, *P. grandiflora* occurs Throughout NE & NY, except for Long Island.

Range: From Newfoundland to New Jersey, westward to the central Great Lakes area; south in the Appalachian Mountains to Georgia.

Nature Notes:

Platanthera shriveri (Shriver's Frilly Orchid) was described as a new species in 2008. Originally known only from the mountains of West Virginia and Virginia, it was discovered in the mountains of New Hampshire in 2011. It is characterized by a longer spur, an upward curving and more deeply-fringed lip, and a blooming time two weeks later than *P. grandiflora*.

Hooker's Orchid
Platanthera hookeri

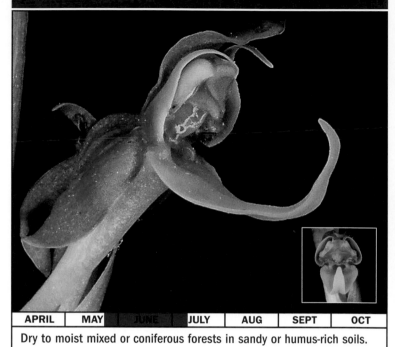

| APRIL | MAY | JUNE | JULY | AUG | SEPT | OCT |

Dry to moist mixed or coniferous forests in sandy or humus-rich soils.

Nature Notes:

Possibly due to climate change, *P. hookeri* appears to be on the decline in NE & NY and is considered extirpated in Connecticut and Rhode Island.

The leaves lay flat and are often obscured by other foliage; it is more easily found after the stalk has risen.

Unlike most orchids, once it matures it often flowers every year.

Noctuid moths have been named as possible pollinators.

The unusual looking flower has been compared to an upraised elephant's trunk, ice tongs, and the face of a gargoyle.

Other Names: Hooker's Rein-Orchid, Pad-leaf Orchid.

Name Origin: The specific name honors Sir William Jackson Hooker (1785–1865) prominent English botanist and professor, and director of London's Royal Botanical Gardens at Kew.

Identification: 4 to 20 inches (10–50 cm) tall.

When not in bloom, the leaves of *Platanthera hookeri* are easily confused with *P. macrophylla* and *P. orbiculata*, the other two species of round-leaved orchids that are often found in the same habitat. The oval leaves of *P. hookeri* are smaller and less glossy and are solid green; the other two species have larger, glossy and

seed
capsules

more rounded leaves that are a pale green underneath. They also have bracts along their stems while *P. hookeri* has none—a feature visible before and after blooming. The yellow-green flowers of *P. hookeri* —with their "ice-tongs" profile—are easily distinguishable from the greenish-white flowers of the other two species, which also bloom later.

Abundance: Rare and local in NE & NY. Although this species occurs infrequently, it can be locally abundant and sometimes forms large colonies in woodlands, where the greenish leaves and flowers blend in with their surroundings.

Range: Manitoba east to Newfoundland, south to Iowa, east to Pennsylvania. Extirpated in Connecticut.

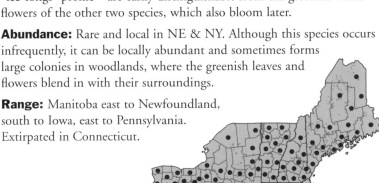

Ragged Fringed Orchid
Platanthera lacera

| APRIL | MAY | JUNE | JULY | AUG | SEPT | OCT |

Wet meadows and marshes, riverbanks, and springy, mucky, herb dominated openings in swamps.

Nature Notes:

The flowers, fragrant in the evening, attract noctuid moths and hawkmoths as pollinators.

Hybridizes with
P. psycodes to form
P. x andrewsii and with
P. grandiflora to form
P. x keenanii.

Often given the title, "least attractive of the fringed orchids" but the flower, with its delicate, thread-like fringes on the lip, is quite beautiful upon close inspection.

Other Names: Green Fringed Orchid, Ragged Orchid.

Name Origin: From the Latin *lacer* meaning "torn" as in "lacerate" (to tear), referring to the deeply fringed lip.

Identification: 8 to 32 inches (20–80 cm) tall.

The flower has a deeply divided, three-lobed lip; each lobe is deeply lacerate-fringed. Easily differentiated from *P. leucophaea* by the deeply shredded fringes of the lip (compare photos of each species).

seed
capsules

Abundance: Occasional throughout, but absent from northernmost New York and Maine.

Range: Manitoba east to Newfoundland, south to Texas and Georgia.

Eastern Prairie Fringed Orchid
Platanthera leucophaea

| APRIL | MAY | JUNE | JULY | AUG | SEPT | OCT |

Rich, black soil of wet prairies and fens.

Nature Notes:

This stunning beauty with tall, full-flowered racemes is one of the premier orchid species of North America. Unfortunately, its habitat is ideal for farming when drained; as a result, the species is federally listed as endangered. Sadly, it is nearly extirpated throughout much of its former range.

At dusk the flowers emit a delicious fragrance that entices its nocturnal sphinx moth pollinators.

A fast-growing orchid which, in suitable soil, can flower in five years from seed.

One of the rarest and most beautiful orchids in our area. Due to the placement of the anthers as eyes, the creamy-white blossoms resemble a strange, fringed face.

Other Names: Prairie Fringed Orchid/Orchis, Prairie White Fringed Orchid/Orchis.

Name Origin: The name, *leucophaea*, is derived from two Greek words: *leucon*, "white," and *phaios*, "gray," referring to the creamy-white color of the blossoms.

Identification: 18 to 47 inches (45–120 cm) tall.

Might be confused with *P. lacera*, our only other white fringed-orchid; but *P. leucophaea* has creamy-white flowers (*P. lacera*'s are greenish-white) a longer nectar spur, and more orderly fringes than *P. lacera*, the "Ragged" Fringed Orchid. It has also been confused with

the white-flowered form of *P. grandiflora*, but the two can easily be differentiated by the shape of the column and nectary opening, as well as the depth of fringing on the lip petal.

Interesting hybrids with *P. lacera* (*P.* x *hollandii*) and *P. psycodes* (*P.* x *reznicekii*) have been recently described from southwestern Ontario. These hybrids are considered to be a threat to the species' survival, because they dilute the genetic purity of the few remaining isolated populations.

Abundance: Extremely rare in New England with one extant population in Aroostook County, Maine. Although numerous historical records exist from western New York, it is considered extirpated there.

Range: Iowa east to Ontario and Maine, south to Oklahoma and Virginia.

The disjunct—and now mostly extirpated— stations in New York, New Jersey, Virginia and Maine are a result of the midwestern prairie moving northeastward following the retreat of the Wisconsin ice sheet during the last ice age.

Goldie's Pad-leaved Orchid
Platanthera macrophylla

| APRIL | MAY | JUNE | JULY | AUG | SEPT | OCT |

Damp, rich humus in deep shade of mixed deciduous & coniferous woods.

Nature Notes:

A truly stunning, otherworldly orchid, and an unforgettable sight when discovered in the deep recesses of their forest redoubt.

The lily-pad-like leaves of *P. macrophylla* can be twice the size of those of *P. orbiculata* and are often the size of dinner plates.

The large, succulent leaves and unique flowers of this species give it an almost tropical appearance.

Other Names: Round-leaf Rein-Orchid, Round-leaved Orchid, Lesser Round-leaf Orchid.

Name Origin: *Macrophylla* is from two Greek words: *macros*, "large" and *phyllon*, "leaf," in reference to the oftentimes large size of the leaves of the variety.

Identification: 10 to 30 inches (12–75 cm) tall.

When not in bloom, the 3 species of round-leaved orchids are very similar. (See *P. orbiculata*, pg. 120 and *P. hookeri*, pg. 110 for further discussion) Originally described as separate species in the early 1800s, orchidologists in the twentieth century—perhaps overwhelmed by the difficulties the two similar species repre-

Note
long
spurs

sented—lumped them together under the name *Habenaria orbiculata*.
Variety *maculata* was used for unusually large specimens of the species.
In 1993 Joyce and Alan Reddoch clarified the similarities and differences
between these two orchids and restored species level recognition to
each. Height and leaf size cannot be relied on for identification,
although *P. macrophylla* is usually larger. Spur length is the major distinguishing characteristic: plants with a spur length of less than 28 mm are
classified as *P. orbiculata*; those with a spur length of 28 mm
or more are *P. macrophylla*.

Abundance: Rare to local in NE & NY; can
form large colonies.

Believed to be extirpated in
Connecticut.

Range: Newfoundland
to Michigan and south
to Pennsylvania.

Blunt-leaf Rein Orchid
Platanthera obtusata subsp. obtusata

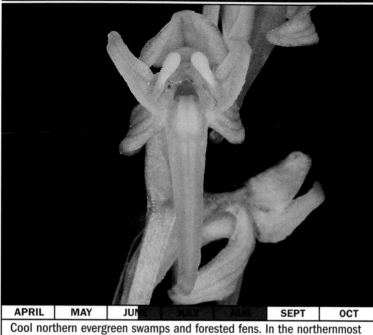

| APRIL | MAY | JUNE | JULY | AUG | SEPT | OCT |

Cool northern evergreen swamps and forested fens. In the northernmost limits of its range it grows on the exposed and treeless arctic tundra.

Nature Notes:

Mosquitoes and small pyralid moths are pollinators. Mosquitoes are sometimes observed flying in the dark forest with pollinia glued to their heads like small headlamps.

Under ideal conditions, it's not unusual to see hundreds of plants within a few feet of one another.

The Eurasian subsp. *oligantha* hybridizes with the North American subsp. *obtusata* in Alaska.

This circumpolar orchid does not grow in the southern part of our region.

Other Names: One-leaved Rein Orchid, Northern Small Bog Orchid, Blunt-leaved Rein Orchid.

Name Origin: From the Latin *obtusatus* meaning "blunt" referring to the blunt tip of the single leaf.

Identification: 6 to 14 inches (15–35 cm) tall; in the forma *collectanea* 2 to 5" (5 to 13 cm) tall.

The single, broadly-blunted leaf raised above the moss or needles makes identification easy.

Abundance: Local in northern NE & NY, rare in MA.

seed
capsules

Range: Alaska east to Newfoundland, south
to Colorado and the upper Great Lakes region,
east to western Massachusetts.

Pad-leaved Orchid
Platanthera orbiculata

APRIL	MAY	JUNE	JULY	AUG	SEPT	OCT

Damp, rich humus in deep shade of mixed deciduous & coniferous woods.

Nature Notes:

Known as "heal-all" by the old-time native mountaineers, the leaves were used in many ways for many ills.

Sphinx and noctuid moths have been documented as pollinators.

The large, succulent leaves and unique flowers of this species give it an almost tropical appearance. It is an unforgettable sight in its deep forest habitat.

Other Names: Round-leaf Rein-Orchid, Round-leaved Orchid, Lesser Round-leaf Orchid

Name Origin: The name, *orbiculata*, is from the Latin word *orbiculatus* meaning "round," in reference to the round leaves.

Identification: 10 to 30 inches (12–75 cm) tall.

When not in bloom, the 3 species of round-leaved orchids are very similar. (See *P. macrophylla*, pg. 116 and *P. hookeri*, pg. 110 for further discussion) Originally described as separate species in the early 1800s, orchidologists in the twentieth century—perhaps overwhelmed by the difficulties the two similar species repre-

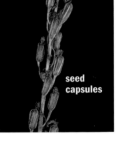

seed capsules

sented—lumped them together under the name *Habenaria orbiculata*. Variety *maculata* was used for unusually large specimens of the species. In 1993 Joyce and Alan Reddoch clarified the similarities and differences between these two orchids and restored species level recognition to each. Height and leaf size cannot be relied on for identification, although *P. macrophylla* is usually larger. Spur length is the major distinguishing characteristic: plants with a spur length of less than 28 mm are classified as *P. orbiculata*; those with a spur length of 28 mm or more are *P. macrophylla*.

Abundance: Rare to local in NE & NY; can form large colonies. Extirpated in CT.

Range: Occurs from southeastern Alaska south to Oregon, east to Newfoundland and south in the Appalachian Mountains to North Carolina.

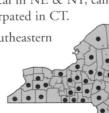

Pale Fringed Orchid
Platanthera pallida

APRIL	MAY	JUNE	JULY	AUG	SEPT	OCT

Restricted to the oldest, most stable Pitch Pine (*Pinus rigida*) stands within sandy, semi-xeric, interdunal hollows.

Nature Notes:

100 years ago, local botanists reported an "unusual" pale yellow orchid from eastern Long Island, NY, similar to, but different from *P. cristata*.

P. pallida does not appear to be a "distinct species" nor is it merely a typical hybrid, as proposed by some botanists; it may be a population in the early stages of evolution.

P. pallida occurs in a near-xeric habitat; *P. cristata*'s habitat is considerably wetter.

This "new species" has been a source of controversy and debate ever since its original description in 1992.

Other Names: Pale Fringed Orchis, Pale Cristata.

Name Origin: *pallida* meaning "pale" referring to the color of the flowers as compared to typical *P. cristata*.

Identification: 12 to 28 inches (30–70 cm) tall.

Very similar to *P. cristata* and reported to differ in shorter spurs, entire dorsal sepals, and lateral sepal and lip orientation; however, some orchid experts include these differences within the morphological range of *P. cristata*.

Hybrids of *P. cristata* with *P. blephariglottis* are *P.* x *canbyi* and look similar to *P. pallida*. Both

seed capsules

parents used to occur near the *P. pallida* locality.

P. pallida is definitely NOT a pale "color form" of *P. cristata* (forma *straminea*).

Abundance: extremely rare, known only from two colonies.

All the flowers on any given *P. pallida* inflorescence always set seed; this may account for the large, but local, colonies.

Range: North American range restricted to the Napeague region of eastern Long Island's South Fork, NY.

Nature Notes:

During the past 5 years, flowering heads of *P. pallida* have been snipped off by some browsers, either deer or cottontail rabbits, or both.

Small Purple Fringed Orchid
Platanthera psycodes

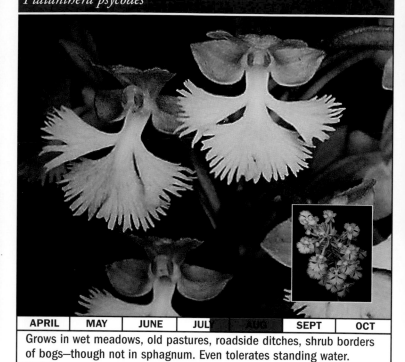

APRIL	MAY	JUNE	JULY	AUG	SEPT	OCT

Grows in wet meadows, old pastures, roadside ditches, shrub borders of bogs—though not in sphagnum. Even tolerates standing water.

Nature Notes:

The differently shaped nectary openings of *P. psycodes* and *P. grandiflora* attract different pollinators, a phenomenon that results in reproductive isolation. The round opening of *P. grandiflora* allows a bumblebee (an "eye-depositing" pollinator) to insert its entire head into the opening, whereas the narrower, dumbbell-shaped opening of *P. psycodes* allows access only to the pro-

Note the dumbell-shaped nectary opening.

The brilliant purple racemes of this very attractive orchid are a welcome sight in high summer.

Other Names: Lesser Purple Fringed-Orchid, Small Purple Fringed Orchis, Butterfly Orchid.

Name Origin: The name, *psycodes*, is from the Greek word *Psyche*, the mythological lover Cupid. *Psyche* became the personification of the human soul; the word also means butterfly, hence one of its common names—Butterfly Orchid.

Identification: Up to 40 inches (100 cm) tall.

Although they appear identical to the untrained eye, *P. psycodes* and *P. grandiflora* are distinguished by differences in column shape and size as well as the shape of the nectary opening (see entry for *P. grandiflora*, pg 108 for more detailed information).

One of our showiest orchids, within a colony

forma
albiflora

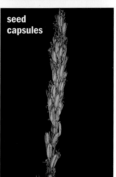

seed
capsules

one is likely to encounter flowers of every shade of color from white (forma *albiflora* inset photo above) to bi-colored, to deep purple.

A very rare hybrid between *P. grandiflora* and *P. psycodes* (*P.* x *enigma*) was described in 2009. Very attractive hybrids with *P. lacera* (*P.* x *andrewsii*) are more common.

Abundance: The commoner of the two purple fringed-orchids in NE & NY, it is relatively frequent and often occurs in large colonies, especially in mountainous areas.

Range: Manitoba east to Newfoundland, south to West Virginia and New Jersey, south in the Appalachian Mountains to Georgia.

boscis of a butterfly or moth. This phenomenon makes *P. psycodes* more efficient reproductively, as the pollinia from *P. grandiflora* tend to fall off the bee's eyes when in flight, and hence more widespread.

Rose Pogonia
Pogonia ophioglossoides

white form
forma
albiflora

APRIL	MAY	JUNE	JULY	AUG	SEPT	OCT

Sphagnum bogs, swamps, wet meadows, pond shores, sphagnous thickets.

Nature Notes:

Rose Pogonia's flowering season usually comes after *Arethusa* and overlaps with *Calopogon*, but in some years all three of these fen loving orchids may be blazing in color at the same time.

Finding a plant with two flowers is a rare treat.

The white-flowered forma *albiflora* appears as a ghost among pink fairies.

Rose Pogonia cannot tolerate much drought and are among the first plants to perish when bogs begin to dry, while their companions, the calopogons with their bulbous corms, may persist.

A delicate jewel of open bogs and meadows where flowers lift their red-bearded heads, like snakes in grass, above the surrounding marshland.

Other Names: Snakemouth Orchid, Goldcrest, Rose Crested Orchid, Snake Mouth, Adder's Mouth, Adder's-tongue-leaved Pogonia, Beard Flower, Crested-ettercap, Ettercap, Rose Crest-lip, Sweet Crest-orchid.

Name Origin: Pogonia: From the Greek *pogon*, meaning "beard" referring to the bearded crest of the lip; *ophioglossoides*: From the Greek *ophis* meaning "snake," *glossa* meaning "tongue," and *eidos* meaning "resembling," hence "resembling the tongue of a snake," but actually referring to the plant's resemblance to the adder's-tongue fern (*Ophioglossum*), with its solitary leaf.

a crab spider waits for prey

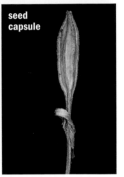

seed capsule

Identification: 8 to 14 inches (20–35 cm) tall.

A single leaf near the middle of the stem distinguishes this species from the similar Dragon's-mouth and Grass-pink. Pure white, very deep-colored, and unusually veined forms occur locally and are characteristic of certain areas. Plant size varies greatly from colony to colony, probably because of environmental factors. Vegetative propagation sometimes produces large colonies.

Abundance: Occasional throughout and locally common.

Range: Manitoba east to Newfoundland, south to Texas and Florida.

Nature Notes:

Though primarily a bog plant in our region, Rose Pogonia also grows in damp, sandy depressions on Long Island, NY, and coastal NE.

Case's Ladies'-Tresses
Spiranthes casei var. casei

APRIL	MAY	JUNE	JULY	AUG	SEPT	OCT

Dry open sites in thin shale or sandy soils; often along roads or in old fields.

Nature Notes:

Spiranthes casei wasn't described until 1974. It had been previously classified as *S. intermedia*—a completely different plant—or erroneously as the "northern phase" of *S. vernalis*—a much more southerly species.

Pollinators include sweat bees (family Halictidae) and bumblebees of the genus *Bombus*.

An uncommon orchid that favors dry, roadside habitats.

Other Names: None.

Name Origin: Honors Frederick W. Case (1927–2011) consummate Michigan botanist and author of *Orchids of the Western Great Lakes Region*, who first realized that the species was not properly classified.

Identification: 3 to 18 inches (8–46 cm) tall.

The small, nodding, partially open flowers with yellow throats in a single row distinguish it from two other species that can occur in the same habitat: *S. cernua* (double row, typically a cream-colored throat, nodding) and *S. ochroleuca* (butterscotch-colored throat, double row). Also, *S. casei* blooms approximately two weeks earlier than the other two species. It

seed
capsules

might also be confused with *S.* x *borealis*, the hybrid between *S. casei* and *S. ochroleuca*, which has a different floral pattern, with more space between the rows.

Abundance: Rare in NE & NY; locally common in the Adirondack Mountains of New York and northern New Hampshire.

Range: Ontario east to Nova Scotia, south to northwestern Minnesota, Wisconsin, east through northern Pennsylvania to western Maine.

Nodding Ladies'-Tresses
Spiranthes cernua

| APRIL | MAY | JUNE | JULY | AUG | SEPT | OCT |

Open moist disturbed areas such as roadside ditches, edges of swampy fields, springs and fens.

Nature Notes:

Spiranthes *cernua* is the most difficult of all North American native orchids to describe concisely. Because it is a compilospecies with one-way incoming gene flow from several other species, plants in different geographic locations resemble the contributing diploid species of that area.

In our area S. *ochroleuca* is the only basic diploid species that contributes gene flow; nonetheless, in some locations the two species blend together, making precise identification a challenge.

The tall racemes with their trumpet-like, crystalline flowers are a beautiful addition to the autumn landscape.

Other Names: Autumn Ladies'-Tresses, Nodding Tresses, Drooping Ladies'-Tresses.

Name Origin: The name, *cernua*, is from the Latin word *cernuus* "faced to the ground," referring to the nodding position of the flowers. It was described by Linnaeus in 1753.

Identification: 4 to 20 inches (10–50 cm) tall.

Very similar to *S. ochroleuca*; so similar that *S. ochroleuca* was at one time treated as a variety of *S. cernua*. There are distinct differences in appearance habitat preference. (See *S. ochroleuca* pg. 136) Typically, *S. ochroleuca* has a distinct butterscotch-colored trough in the center of the lip that is visible from the bot-

top view

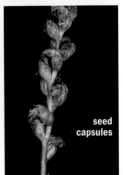

seed capsules

tom of the lip as well. *Spiranthes cernua* favors the wetter parts of roadside shoulders; *S. ochroleuca* prefers the drier portions of the same areas and is slightly later blooming. Another species sometimes found in the same area, *S. casei*, features small, nodding, partially open flowers with yellow throats in a single row. In contrast, *S. cernua* has a double row of flowers and typically a cream-colored throat.

Nature Notes:

Pollinated by bees, including *Bombus*, it also reproduces asexually without fertilization by producing plantlets via spreading rhizomes, which can produce distinct local races.

Abundance: The most commonly encountered Spiranthes in NE & NY. In early autumn large numbers may be found, often along roadsides, especially in the western Adirondack Mountains of New York and the White Mountains of New Hampshire.

Range: South Dakota east to Nova Scotia, south to Texas and Florida.

Northern Slender Ladies'-Tresses
Spiranthes lacera var. lacera
Southern Slender Ladies'-Tresses
Spiranthes lacera var. gracilis

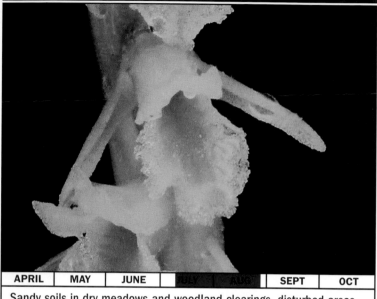

APRIL	MAY	JUNE	JULY	AUG	SEPT	OCT

Sandy soils in dry meadows and woodland clearings, disturbed areas.

Nature Notes:

Spiranthes lacera is pollinated by bumblebees and other small bees.

The two varieties overlap in all of NE & NY—except for Maine— and in many populations the variety is easy to determine. But other populations occur where both varieties and every possible combination between the two exist.

Unlike most orchids, reaches flowering size in 3 to 5 years, creating new populations quickly.

A dainty orchid notable for its green "throat."

Other Names: Slender Ladies'-Tresses.

Name Origin: The name, *lacera*, is a Latin word meaning "torn," *gracilis* is Latin for "thin," referring to the slender, wand-like stem.

Identification: 4 to 18 inches (10–46 cm) tall.

This is the only *Spiranthes* species in our area with a green lip. The two varieties are distinct in pure populations, but the occurrence of intermediary forms can cause frustration. In var. *lacera* the lower flowers are well spaced out on the inflorescence, resulting in a loose spiral with moderate pubescence; var. *gracilis* has a denser, oftentimes multi-ranked spiral with no pubescence. Variety *lacera* blooms a little earlier than var. *gracilis*.

Abundance: Both varieties are locally common throughout NE & NY.

Range: Variety *lacera*: Alberta east to Nova Scotia, south to Missouri and Virginia; var. *gracilis*: Michigan east to Nova Scotia and Maine, south to Kansas, Texas and Georgia.

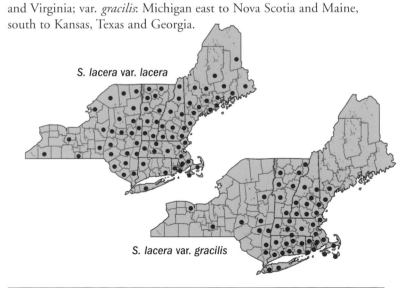

Shining Ladies'-Tresses
Spiranthes lucida

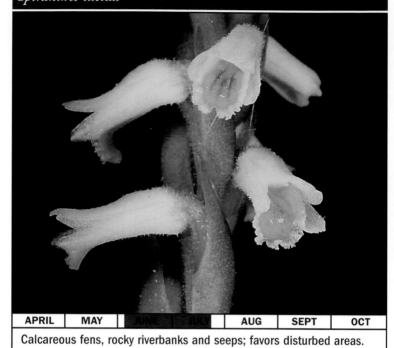

| APRIL | MAY | JUNE — JULY | AUG | SEPT | OCT |

Calcareous fens, rocky riverbanks and seeps; favors disturbed areas.

Nature Notes:

May be more overlooked than rare, due to its habit of growing hidden amongst grasses and swamp vegetation.

Spiranthes lucida is specifically adapted to pollination by short-tongued halictid bees. The nectar is secreted onto the front of the column rather than into the base of the floral tube, where it is more easily reached by a short-tongued bee.

The earliest blooming of our Ladies'-Tresses, notable for its distinctive saffron colored lip.

Other Names: Shampoo Orchid, Wide-leaved Ladies'-Tresses.

Name Origin: The name, *lucida*, is derived from the Latin word *lucidus*, meaning "bright," or "shining," referring to the glossy quality of the leaves.

Identification: 3 to 11 inches (8–28 cm) tall.

Impossible to confuse with any other *Spiranthes*, due to its early blooming date, lemon yellow lip and distinctive shiny leaves. Even when not in flower, it is an attractive plant with its distinctive rosette of broad, sleek, green leaves. It is the only species of *Spiranthes* where the leaves remain green and

functioning after flowering; in the other species a new rosette of leaves forms in the late fall.

Abundance: Rare to locally abundant in NE & NY. Extirpated in Rhode Island.

Range: Wisconsin and Iowa east to Nova Scotia, south to Nebraska, east to Virginia.

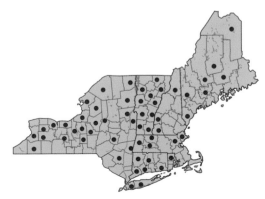

Yellow Ladies'-Tresses
Spiranthes ochroleuca

| APRIL | MAY | JUNE | JULY | AUG | SEPT | OCT |

Dry or well drained soils along roadsides and woodland clearings & edges.

Nature Notes:

Spiranthes ochroleuca is probably the latest blooming orchid in NE & NY.

Initially described in 1901, the identity of this orchid has long been the subject of great controversy. A species to some, a variety to others, and ignored altogether by most! Many botanists assumed that S. *ochroleuca* was simply one of the variations of S. *cernua*.

It is pollinated by bumblebees.

A stately roadside orchid with a distinct butterscotch-colored throat.

Other Names: Yellow Nodding Ladies'-Tresses.

Name Origin: The name, *ochroleuca*, is from two Greek words: *ochros* "pale yellow" and *leucos* "white," referring to the yellowish-white color of the flowers.

Identification: 6 to 20 inches (15–50 cm) tall.

Very closely related to *S. cernua* (see pg 130) but is differentiated by the distinct butterscotch-colored trough in the center of the lip—that is visible from the bottom of the lip as well—and the ascending (as opposed to nodding) flowers and lateral sepals. Also, the spike is proportionately longer and narrower

seed
capsules

and the flowers are more widely spaced than *S. cernua*. It also favors drier habitats.

Abundance: Occasional throughout NE & NY except for northern Maine.

Range: Michigan east to Nova Scotia, south to Kentucky and South Carolina.

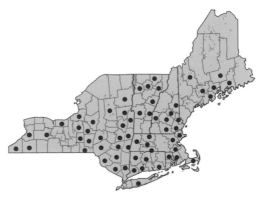

Hooded Ladies'-Tresses
Spiranthes romanzoffiana

APRIL	MAY	JUNE	JU...	...AUG...	SEPT	OCT

Wet sedge meadows, ditches, seeps, usually calcareous soils.

Nature Notes:

This is the most widespread *Spiranthes* in North America. It is believed to have spread eastward along the migratory paths of Brant Geese and other sea birds to England, Ireland and Scotland (where it is uncommon) via seed carried by these birds.

In a few areas it hybridizes with *Spiranthes lacera* var. *lacera* to produce *S.* x *simpsonii*.

Pollinators include halictid bees and bumblebees.

An elegant late-summer orchid.

Other Names: Oval Ladies'-Tresses, Irish Ladies-Tresses (in Europe).

Name Origin: Named by German botanist Adelbert von Chamisso in honor of Nicholas Romanzoff, a Russian diplomat, patron and financial supporter of scientific expeditions.

Identification: 4 to 20 inches (10–50 cm) tall.

The hood formed by the sepals and petals over the tightly constricted, downward facing, fiddle-shaped lip distinguish this species from the other *Spiranthes* in our area. This lip has been compared to a face with a receding chin. Its faintly vanilla-scented flowers are also distinctive. Superficially, it resembles *S. cernua*, but the spike is narrower and more tapering. The slightly pubescent flower spike is usually

crowded and so tightly coiled that it produces three ranks of creamy-white flowers.

Abundance: Locally common in northern calcareous fens in NE & NY; very rare southward.

Range: Widespread and transcontinental: from Alaska east to Newfoundland, south to California, northern New Mexico, Indiana, and east to Maine, also Great Britain and Ireland.

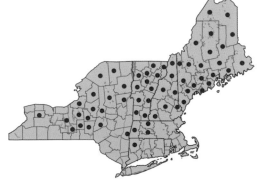

Little Ladies'-Tresses
Spiranthes tuberosa

APRIL	MAY	JUNE	JULY	AUG	SEPT	OCT

Dry sandy to rocky soils in old fields, roadsides and open woodlands.

Nature Notes:

This minute species is very difficult to see in its native habitat, which may account for its presumed rarity.

Best viewed under magnification; as in many orchids, the flower's cellular tissue appears to be composed of rounded, polished crystals, a condition that has been called "jewelaceous."

It is pollinated by small bees and other small insects.

Despite its size, *S. tuberosa* is one of our most attractive and irresistible orchids, with its graceful spire of tiny, jewel-like crystalline flowers.

Other Names: Beck's Tresses, Little Pearl-twist, White Spiraled-Orchid.

Name Origin: The name, *tuberosa*, is from the Latin word *tuberosus* "tuberous," referring to the solitary swollen root characteristic of the species.

Identification: 5 to 12 inches (13–30 cm) tall.

Spiranthes tuberosa is easily recognized by its pure white flowers, midsummer blooming time and absence of leaves during flowering. An elongated, vertical, tuberous root is produced annually. A rosette of two or three small, ovate leaves appear in the fall and often-

seed
capsules

times persist through the winter. The spike is small, very slender and totally glabrous and produces, in a loose spiral, the smallest flowers (one-eighth inch long or less) of the genus in the eastern United States and Canada.

Abundance: Rare to occasional in NE & NY.

Range: Massachusetts south to central Florida, west to Texas, north to Michigan; throughout the Deep South states.

Grass-leaved Ladies'-Tresses
Spiranthes vernalis

APRIL	MAY	JUNE	JULY	AUG	SEPT	OCT

Damp to moist roadsides and meadows.

Nature Notes:

It is pollinated by small bees and other small insects.

A bundle of fleshy, elongated perennial roots supports the annual vegetation above. Well-established plants may reproduce by stolons, producing clusters of three to four sturdy stems.

A very robust species; specimens 36-plus inches tall with over 50 blossoms have been recorded.

A tall, vigorous summer orchid with flowers up to one-half inch long.

Other Names: Spring Ladies'-Tresses, Linear leaved Ladies'-Tresses, Narrow-leaved Tresses, Spring Tresses.

Name Origin: The name, *vernalis*, is from the Latin word *vernalis* "belonging to spring," referring to the time of year in which it flowers in the southeastern United States.

Identification: 6 to 34 inches (10–85 cm) tall.

Plants vary greatly in size and vigor as well as degree of spiraling; flower color is also variable, ranging from nearly pure white to cream with a contrasting yellow lip. The most consistent distinguishing characteristic is the presence in the inflorescence of copious pointed hairs—best visible with a hand lens—which distin-

guishes *S. vernalis* from other species. The leaves of the plant are grass-like.

Abundance: Primarily grows along the coastal areas of NE & NY, isolated populations are not unusual inland. Populations on some of the barrier islands can number in the thousands.

Range: Nebraska south to Texas, east to Florida, north to southern New Hampshire.

Nature Notes:

The specific name, *vernalis*, or "spring," is misleading in New England and New York where it blooms primarily in August.

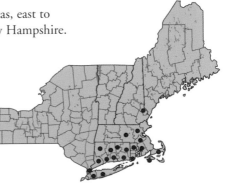

Crane-fly Orchid
Tipularia discolor

APRIL	MAY	JUNE	JULY	AUG	SEPT	OCT

Deep humus or sandy soils of deciduous forests, with Beech.

Nature Notes:

The flowers of *Tipularia* are unique among North American orchids in that they are not bilaterally symmetrical, instead the flowers are lopsided.

When in flower, the solitary leaf is withered.

The best way to find these elusive plants is to do some midwinter scouting in the woods, when the single leaf is most apparent.

Because of its subdued colors, thin stem, and preference for dark woods, this orchid is hard to find during its midsummer bloom.

The cluster of loose flowers resembles a swarm of small craneflies hovering about a foot above the forest floor.

Other Names: Crippled Crane-fly, Elfin-spur, Mottled Crane-fly.

Name Origin: From the Latin *discolor* meaning "two colors" referring to the two colors of the winter leaf: green on top and magenta purple underneath.

Identification: 10 to 20 inches (25–50 cm) tall.

One of only two orchids in our region that has a winter leaf but no leaf when it blooms. The other orchid is Putty-root with a much larger leaf and striking white parallel veining over its entire length.

seed capsules

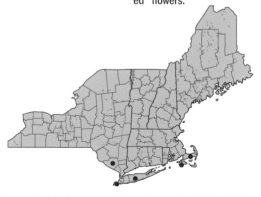

Abundance: very rare and local on eastern Long Island, NY, and southeastern MA.

Range: eastern Texas northeastward to southern Michigan and east to southeastern Massachusetts and south to Florida.

Nature Notes:

The pollinators, nocturnal moths called millers, have pollinaria attached to their right eye when visiting "right-handed" flowers, and to their left eye when visiting "left-handed" flowers.

Three Birds Orchid (Nodding Pogonia)
Triphora trianthophora

APRIL	MAY	JUNE	JULY	AUG	SEPT	OCT

Rich humus in deciduous and mixed woodlands, primarily in beech forests.

Nature Notes:

Four species of *Triphora* exhibit the phenomenon known as thermoperiodicity, where temperature fluctuations are the triggering stimulus to the mass flowering of a species, usually in several waves a week or so apart. As the season progresses, some buds cease developing as if on cue and wait for the less mature buds to catch up. On the appointed day, all the mature buds open simultaneously.

Producing an optimum number of ephemeral flowers on the same day undoubtedly increases the chance of cross-pollination occurring.

An elusive and beautiful woodland orchid whose blossoms last less than one day

Other Names: Nodding-crest, Nodding-cap, Nodding-ettercap, Pendulous Pogonia.

Name Origin: The name, *trianthophora*, is from the Greek *tri*—"threefold," *anthos*—"flower," and *phoros*—"bearing" referring to the common number of flowers seen in the inflorescence at one time; one in bud, one in flower and one fading.

Identification: 4 to 11 inches (8–28 cm) tall.

The stunning flowers of *Triphora* last only one day, opening in mid-morning and closing by mid-afternoon, leaving only a few hours to be observed. Due to its unique flowering habits and woodland habitat, the Three Birds Orchid cannot be confused with any other species.

seed
capsule
and seeds

Abundance: Rare and local throughout NE & NY, and variable due to its biology.

Triphora lives underground saprophytically in symbiosis with its associated root fungus most of the time and only blooms in years when the environmental conditions are right. It may produce only a handful of plants one year and carpet the woods the next, posing a great a challenge to the orchid hunter.

Range: Texas north to Wisconsin east to Maine and south to Florida.

Nature Notes:

Orchid researchers learned that a few degrees decrease in the average night temperature is followed 48 hours later by the mass flowering of all the colonies in that meteorological region.

Glossary

Anther: Part of stamen that holds the pollen.

Acid: Having a pH less than 7.

Alkaline: Having a pH more than 7.

Alternate: Leaves attaching at successively different levels on stem.

Angiosperm: A plant producing flowers and bearing seeds in an ovary.

Auricle: A small earlike projection from the base of a leaf or petal.

Basal: From the base of the plant.

Bog: A wet, acidic, nutrient-poor peatland characterized by sphagnum mosses, shrubs and sedges that receives nutrients only from precipitation.

Boreal: Far northern latitudes.

Bract: Accessory structure at base of some flowers, appearing leaf-like.

Bulblet: Small bulb borne above the ground.

Bulbils: A small bulb that develops from an aerial bud Bulbils are easily detached and function as a means of vegetative propagation.

Calcareous: Containing calcium carbonate, or calcite, chalky, with a pH greater than 7.

Capsule: A dry fruit which opens, when the seeds are ripe, at several slits or holes Any closed vessel containing spores or seeds.

Circumboreal: Refers to species distribution which circles the earth's boreal regions.

Clasping: Leaves that partially encircle the stem at the base.

Cleistogamous: Type of flower that remains closed and is self-pollinating (see Autumn Coralroot). Fertilization takes place in unopened flower.

Column: The unique reproductive structure in an orchid flower, consisting of fused stamens and pistils.

Cordate: Shaped like a heart.

Corm: A thickened underground stem.

Corolla: The petals collectively.

Disjunct: Separated, as a population of some plant occurring at considerable remove from the remaining distribution of that taxon.

Dorsal: Above or upper.

Duff: Forest-floor covering composed of decaying leaves, needles, etc.

Endemic: Found only in one region and nowhere else.

Epiphyte: A plant that grows on another plant, usually a tree in the case of orchids, without being parasitic.

Extirpated: Extinct in a certain geographic area like a state, but still exists in other locations.

Fen: An open or treed wetland characterized by a more alkaline source of ground water than a bog.

Glabrous: Smooth Without hair or down.

Inflorescence: The part of the plant with flowers, single or multiple The major orchid inflorescence forms include spike, raceme and scape.

Labellum: Lip, particularly that of an orchid.

Lip: A petal, usually of quite different shape and size to the others, normally at the bottom of the flower, or apparently so, and often, especially in orchids, of complicated structure.

Mesic: A moist and rich habitat.

Monocotyledon: With a single cotyledon or seed-leaf.

Monotypic: A genus that contain only one species.

Mycorrhizal: Symbiotic association between a fungus and plant roots.

Mycotrophic: Describing a symbiotic association between a fungus and the whole of a plant. Such an association occurs when a mycorrhizal fungus extends into the aerial parts of a plant, as in certain orchids.

Non-resupinate: Lip petal in uppermost position, as in *Calopogon tuberosus* for example. Non-resupinate orchid flowers normally position the lip at the bottom just above the column. Some genera, however, such as *Malaxis*, position the lip uppermost with the column below making the flower appear to be up-side-down.

Ovary: The part of the pistil containing the ovules.

Ovate: Egg-shaped.

pH: A term used to express the degree of acidity or alkalinity. Measured on a scale from 0 to 14 with 7 being neutral.

Pedicel: The stem that supports a flower; can be either the main stem or smaller stems attaching multiple flowers to the main stem.

Pistil: The female, seed-producing organ of the flower, in orchids the pistil is part of the column.

Pollinium; pl. Pollinia Coherent masses or 'packets' of pollen. Orchids have two, four, six or eight pollinium (packets) The number of pollinia is one of the major factors in defining a genus of an orchid.

Pseudobulb: Thickened or bulb-like stems (called "pseudobulbs" because they are not true bulbs) produced by some orchids to store water and food Only orchids whose habitat has seasonal periods of dryness or drought have adopted this life-saving characteristic.

Pubescent: Hairy, the hairs short, soft and downy.

Raceme: An elongated stem of multiple flowers with each floret attached by a short stem of its own.

Reflexed: Bent backward abruptly.

Resupinate: Lip petal in lowermost position on flower, the normal position in most orchids.

Reticulate: Network of veins or resembling a net, usually a different color than the leaf.

Rhizome: The woody parts of the rootstock at the base of the orchid which grows along or just under the surface of the ground or along host.

Rosette: A basal cluster of leaves.

Rostellum: A slender extension from upper edge of stigma in orchids.

Saprophyte: Plants often lacking chlorophyll; receiving nourishment from dead or decaying organic matter; needing the services of certain fungi to be able to absorb food.

Scape: The leafless stem of a solitary flower or inflorescence.

Sepal: The outermost whorl of flower segments.

Sheath: The tubular base of the leaf surrounding the flower spike.

Spike: elongate stem of flowers; each floret attached directly to stem.

Stamen: Male part of flower consisting of filament and anther, in orchids the stamen is part of the column.

Stigma: The part of the pistil, usually sticky, that receives the pollen.

Symbiotic: Mutually beneficial.

Tuber: Thickened, subterranean branch having numerous buds or eyes.

Tubercle: A small knobby prominence.

Tuberous: Tuber-like; furnished with tubers.

Variety: Plant having minor characters or variations which separates it from the type species (var.).

Vegetative: Part of a plant not directly concerned with reproduction as the stem and leaves.

Whorl: Three or more leaves, sepals or petals arranged in a circle about an axis.

Xeric: Perennially dry habitat.

Photo Credits

The vast majority of the photos in this guide were taken by co-author Tom Nelson—including the cover images. Check out more of Tom's stunning images at **http://www.pbase.com/tomdean/**...or Google "*tom nelson orchids*." We at Kollath-Stensaas filled in a few holes with images from the following talented photographers.

[Photos are numbered by page and then by location clockwise from top left, starting with A.]

Sylvain Beausejour [www.orchideequebec.com]: 93C

Jim Fowler [http://www.flickr.com/photos/22032600@N04/]: 11 BOTTOM, 74, 75A, 75B, 133 INSET A, 142, 143A, 143B, 146, 147A, 147B, 147C

Lorne Heshka: 47A

Johanna Nelson: 24, 25A, 25B

Kim & Cindy Risen [www.naturescapetours.com]: 3A, 18A, 30, 41E, 46 INSET, 47D, 51C, 70, 88 INSET, 89D, 105C, 119C, 126 INSET

Eleanor "Sam" Saulys: 42 INSET

Scott Shriver: 37C

Sparky Stensaas [www.ThePhotoNaturalist.com]: 3B, 3C

Charles Ufford: 128, 129A, 129B, 136, 137A

Checklist of the Orchids of New England & New York

❏ *Amerorchis rotundifolia*	Small Round-leaved Orchid
❏ *Aplectrum hyemale*	Puttyroot (Adam-and-Eve)
❏ *Arethusa bulbosa*	Dragon's-mouth (Arethusa)
❏ *Calopogon tuberosus var. tuberosus*	Tuberous Grass-Pink
❏ *Calypso bulbosa var. americana*	Calypso (Eastern Fairy Slipper)
❏ *Coeloglossum viride var. virescens*	Long-bracted Orchid
❏ *Corallorhiza maculata var. maculata*	Spotted Coralroot
❏ *Corallorhiza maculata var. occidentalis*	Spotted Coralroot
❏ *Corallorhiza odontorhiza var. odontorhiza*	Autumn Coralroot
❏ *Corallorhiza odontorhiza var. pringlei*	Pringle's Autumn Coralroot
❏ *Corallorhiza striata var. striata*	Striped Coralroot
❏ *Corallorhiza trifida*	Early Coralroot
❏ *Cypripedium acaule*	Pink Lady's-slipper
❏ *Cypripedium arietinum*	Ram's-head Lady's-slipper
❏ *Cypripedium candidum*	Small White Lady's-slipper
❏ *Cypripedium parviflorum var. makasin*	Small N. Yellow Lady's-slipper
❏ *Cypripedium parviflorum var. parviflorum*	Small S. Yellow Lady's-slipper
❏ *Cypripedium parviflorum var. pubescens*	Large Yellow Lady's-slipper
❏ *Cypripedium reginae*	Showy Lady's-slipper
❏ *Epipactis helleborine*	Broad-leaved Helleborine
❏ *Galearis spectabilis*	Showy Orchis
❏ *Goodyera oblongifolia*	Giant Rattlesnake Plantain
❏ *Goodyera pubescens*	Downy Rattlesnake Plantain
❏ *Goodyera repens*	Lesser Rattlesnake Plantain
❏ *Goodyera tesselata*	Checkered Rattlesnake Plantain
❏ *Isotria medeoloides*	Small Whorled Pogonia
❏ *Isotria verticillata*	Large Whorled Pogonia
❏ *Liparis liliifolia*	Lily-leaved Twayblade
❏ *Liparis loeselii*	Loesel's Twayblade
❏ *Listera auriculata*	Auricled Twayblade
❏ *Listera australis*	Southern Twayblade
❏ *Listera convallarioides*	Broad-lipped Twayblade
❏ *Listera cordata var. cordata*	Heart-leaved Twayblade

❏ *Malaxis bayardii* — Bayard's Adder's-mouth
❏ *Malaxis monophyllos var. brachypoda* — White Adder's-mouth
❏ *Malaxis unifolia* — Green Adder's-mouth
❏ *Platanthera aquilonis* — Northern Green Bog-Orchid
❏ *Platanthera blephariglottis var. blephariglottis* — Northern White Fringed Orchid
❏ *Platanthera ciliaris* — Yellow Fringed Orchid
❏ *Platanthera (Gymnadeniopsis) clavellata* — Club-spur Orchid
❏ *Platanthera cristata* — Orange Crested Orchid
❏ *Platanthera dilatata var. dilatata* — White Bog Orchid (Bog Candles)
❏ *Platanthera flava var. herbiola* — Northern Tubercled Orchid
❏ *Platanthera grandiflora* — Large Purple Fringed Orchid
❏ *Platanthera hookeri* — Hooker's Orchid
❏ *Platanthera huronensis* — Green Bog-Orchid
❏ *Platanthera lacera* — Ragged Fringed Orchid
❏ *Platanthera leucophaea* — Eastern Prairie Fringed Orchid
❏ *Platanthera macrophylla* — Goldie's Pad-leaved Orchid
❏ *Platanthera obtusata subsp. obtusata* — Blunt-leaf Rein Orchid
❏ *Platanthera orbiculata* — Pad-leaved Orchid
❏ *Platanthera pallida* — Pale Fringed Orchid
❏ *Platanthera psycodes* — Small Purple Fringed Orchid
❏ *Pogonia ophioglossoides* — Rose Pogonia
❏ *Spiranthes casei var. casei* — Case's Ladies'-Tresses
❏ *Spiranthes cernua* — Nodding Ladies'-Tresses
❏ *Spiranthes lacera var. lacera* — Northern Slender Ladies'-Tresses
❏ *Spiranthes lacera var. gracilis* — Southern Slender Ladies'-Tresses
❏ *Spiranthes lucida* — Shining Ladies'-Tresses
❏ *Spiranthes ochroleuca* — Yellow Ladies'-Tresses
❏ *Spiranthes romanzoffiana* — Hooded Ladies'-Tresses
❏ *Spiranthes tuberosa* — Little Ladies'-Tresses
❏ *Spiranthes vernalis* — Grass-leaved Ladies'-Tresses
❏ *Tipularia discolor* — Crane-fly Orchid
❏ *Triphora trianthophora* — Three Birds Orchid

Favorite Orchid Hunting Sites

Unlike some parts of North America where native orchids are more frequent, most orchid sites in our area are by necessity kept secret due to declining populations of many species. A good way to locate orchids is to watch for suitable habitat; many species favor limestone areas, and fens and bogs can also be productive. Many orchids colonize disturbed areas such as roadsides and old fields—watch these areas carefully. Although pockets of good orchid habitat exist in all of New England and New York, the boreal forest zone in the northern parts of Maine, Vermont and New Hampshire is especially orchid-rich. Some information can be made available to assist in the search for these elusive beauties. Happy hunting!

The Nature Conservancy has many preserves in our area and many of them offer good orchid hunting possibilities. Click on the individual states on the website below and then click on "Places We Protect." http://www.nature.org/ourinitiatives/regions/northamerica/unitedstates/index.htm

MAINE
53 species and varieties
Aroostook County

Although suitable orchid habitat occurs throughout Maine, Aroostook County—the premier orchid county in all of New England and New York with 42 species of wild orchids documented—is unrivaled for orchid hunting. The large tracts of untouched land combined with cool Northern White Cedar swamps and numerous calcareous bogs make it an orchid lover's paradise. Spring arrives in June in this area, so trips in either late June-early July and again in mid-August will be rewarding. Most of the orchids are found in two areas: the Crystal Bog region in southwestern Aroostook County and the Caribou-Fort Kent region further north.

Crystal Bog

Because of its size, this species-rich area is known locally as 10,000-Acre Bog. Although orchids occur in the entire area, there are several fens where the orchids are most prolific. The Nature Conservancy owns much of Crystal Bog and due to the sensitive nature of the habitat, these areas are not open to the public and permission must be obtained in advance to enter. Two of the protected fens harbor the only remaining populations of *Platanthera leucophaea* in New England and New

York. The largest population of Arethusa in New England and New York is found in Crystal Bog; Calypso, three species of Lady's-slippers, Coralroot, Twayblade, Adder's-mouth, Large Round-leaved Orchid, White and Purple Fringed Orchids and Northern Slender Ladies'-Tresses are some of the other orchids that can be found during a typical season. There are some areas of the bog that are open to the public: the six-mile Patten to Sherman Multi-Use Trail provides an opportunity to explore for orchids as it passes through Crystal Bog. For map and info: http://www.goby.com/sherman-to-patten-trail--near--patten-me/e-11341520#source=maine.gov

Caribou/Fort Kent
The other species-rich area is in northern Aroostook County. Following US 1 from Caribou north to Fort Kent and then west to Allagash leads to some of the most remote but accessible botanical areas in New England and New York. Blooming about ten days later than the Crystal area, most of the same species can be found in the forests, bogs and fens that abound in the area. Yellow Lady's-slippers are frequent in the woods and can sometimes be seen from the road. Two orchids have their only New England and New York stations here: the Giant Rattlesnake Plantain and the Small Round-leaved Orchid. This is also a good area to search for the elusive Auricled Twayblade.

NEW HAMPSHIRE
54 species and varieties
Coos County
Coos County, in northern New Hampshire, has many calcareous shale deposits and damp roadside meadows that offer good orchid habitat. Case's, Nodding, Yellow, Northern Slender, and Hooded Ladies'-Tresses are all found along the roadsides around Colebrook , with the later two blooming in early August and the first three around Labor Day. Numerous Small and Large Purple Fringed Orchids frequent damp roadsides in the area in mid-summer. Large colonies of hundreds of Pink Lady's-slippers adorn the hillsides along Hwy 112 (the Kancamagus Highway) just east of Lincoln, further south in the White Mountains.

Hurlbert Swamp Preserve
Located in Coos County near Stewartstown, this 313 acre Nature Conservancy Preserve protects a remarkable 10,000 year old high-elevation Northern White Cedar-Balsam Fir swamp. Northern White Cedar is a boreal species that is at the southern limit of its range in this location. Long known for its rare orchids and birds, the preserve features a

one-mile bog bridge trail complete with a boardwalk to protect the fragile habitat. Yellow Lady's-slippers and Long-bracted Orchid are amongst the species present. For directions and info:
http://www.nature.org/ourinitiatives/regions/northamerica/united-states/newhampshire/placesweprotect/hurlbert-swamp.xml

Mt. Teneriffe Preserve

This 170-acre Nature Conservancy Preserve, located in southeastern New Hampshire near Milton, is home to the globally threatened Small Whorled Pogonia, a notoriously capricious species that can lie dormant for years. There is a 1.6-mile loop trail that offers beautiful views and interesting woodlands if one is not lucky enough to find the orchid!
http://www.nature.org/ourinitiatives/regions/northamerica/united-states/newhampshire/placesweprotect/mt.-teneriffe-preserve,-milton.xml

VERMONT
57 species and varieties
Eshqua Bog Natural Area

Located near Hartland, Eshqua Bog is a 40-acre Nature Conservancy preserve that protects an 8-acre wetland abounding in Showy Lady's-slippers—at least several hundred—that are usually in prime-bloom around June 20th. Fewer numbers of Large Yellow Lady's-slippers bloom about two weeks earlier; Northern Green and Tall White Bog Orchids and Long-bracted Orchid also occur at Eshqua Bog. A 200-foot boardwalk is the centerpiece of a one-mile trail system. For information and directions: http://www.newfs.org/visit/sanctuaries/eshqua-bog-natural-area-hartland-vt.html

Northeast Kingdom

Many species of orchids grow on the slopes of Mt. Pisgah on the eastern side of the spectacularly beautiful Lake Willoughby, located in the fabled Northeast Kingdom, where due to the presence of limestone and calcareous shale, a lot of good orchid habitat can be found. The South Trail up Mt. Pisgah, which can be accessed from the main parking lot at the south end of the lake, is a good place to search. Four species of Lady's-slippers, Coralroots, Twayblades, Adder's-Mouths, Round-Leaved Orchids, Bog Orchids and Ladies'-Tresses have been found there. These species of course do not all bloom at the same time and visits in late May–early June, mid–July, and late August–early September are recommended to catch the different blooming waves.
http://www.hikenewengland.com/Pisgah040605.html

NEW YORK
65 species and varieties
The Adirondack Mountains

While not as orchid-rich as some parts of northern New England, some species can be found in the black spruce bogs, fens and boreal forests of the Adirondack Mountains and surrounding areas.

Paul Smith's College Visitor Interpretive Center

Located in the heart of the Adirondacks near Saranac Lake, five species of orchids can be viewed along the "Boreal Life Trail" which features a boardwalk through a black spruce swamp. The preserve is known for its large population of White Fringed Orchids; other species present are: Rose Pogonia, Checkered and Lesser Rattlesnake Plantain and Broadleaf Helleborine. For information:
http://www.adirondackvic.org/BorealLife.html

In the autumn thousands of Nodding Ladies'-Tresses, as well as scattered populations of Cases' and Yellow Nodding Ladies'-Tresses can be found in the southern Adirondacks along Rt. 10 north of the tiny town of Pine Lake, and Rt. 29A west of Pine Lake.

The limestone alvars and woodlands approaching Lake Ontario in the western Adirondacks yield small populations of Ram's-head, Yellow and Showy Lady's-slippers; there are several Nature Conservancy Preserves in this area worth exploring.

Central New York State

This is a large area stretching from Utica to just west of Rochester and south to Corning and Binghamton. Limestone areas and calcareous fens are frequent and provide lots of good orchid habitat.

Bergen Swamp Preserve and Zurich Bog

Located southwest of Rochester a marl fen in this preserve harbors one of the few remaining populations of Small White Lady's-slippers to be found in New England and New York. Yellow Lady's-slippers, as well as their hybrids with the Small White Lady's-slippers, occur there as well. Pink Lady's-slippers, Long-bracted Orchid, Early Coralroot, and Shining Ladies'-Tresses are some of the other orchid species that can be found in the rich woods at Bergen.

Zurich Bog is located east of Rochester and has populations of Yellow and Showy Lady's-slippers. The elusive Southern Twayblade occurs there, as well as Coralroot, Rattlesnake Plantain and Large Whorled Pogonia. Information and maps for both preserves can be obtained on the Bergen Swamp Preservation Society website:
http://www.bergenswamp.org/

Labrador Hollow Unique Area
Located on the borders of Cortland and Onondaga Counties, Labrador Hollow features a boardwalk nature trail through a wetland area. Several orchid species—including Yellow Lady's-slipper and Heart-leaved Twayblade—can be found in the woods and fens of the preserve. http://www.cnyhiking.com/LabradorHollowUniqueArea.htm

Nelson Swamp
Located in Madison County southeast of Syracuse, Nelson Swamp preserves a White Cedar swamp and has long been of interest to botanists because of the rich diversity of its plant life. 400 species of vascular plants have been catalogued within the preserve. The endangered Striped Coralroot, Showy Lady's-slipper and Small Purple Fringed Orchid are just three of the species known to occur at Nelson Swamp. http://www.dec.ny.gov/lands/8150.html

New York City/Long Island
Surprisingly, 9 species of orchids can still be found within the five boroughs of New York City: Autumn Coralroot, Downy Rattlesnake Plantain, Large Whorled Pogonia, Pink Lady's-slipper, Loesel's Twayblade, Ragged Fringed Orchid, Nodding, Southern Slender and Little Ladies'-Tresses (list courtesy of Dave Taft, NPS). Although no native orchids remain in Manhattan, the increasingly widespread non-native Broadleaf Helleborine has established itself in Inwood Hill Park on the northern tip of the island. Luckily there are thousands of acres of preserved parkland in the outer boroughs where isolated pockets of suitable habitat have survived.

The urban sprawl of New York City has thankfully not reached the eastern end of Long Island, where there are some excellent orchid hunting possibilities. Pink Lady's-slippers—sometimes accompanied by Large Whorled Pogonia—are common in the sandy oak woods and pitch pine habitat that predominates. Rose Pogonia and Tuberous Grass-Pink are frequent along the Walking Dunes Trail in Hither Hills State Park on the east side of Napeague Harbor. The endemic and very rare Pale Fringed Orchid can also be found in the vicinity, growing in interdunal hollows under pitch pine.

Connetquot River State Park Preserve
A former private hunting preserve that was a favorite haunt of the Whitneys and Vanderbilts in the late nineteenth and early twentieth centuries, this 3,473 acre state park gives one an idea what Long Island looked like before it was settled. It harbors Pink Lady's-slippers, the very rare Southern Twayblade, Orange Crested Orchid and Northern White Fringed Orchid. http://nysparks.com/parks/8/details.aspx

MASSACHUSETTS
54 species and varieties
Metropolitan Boston

The Greater Boston area has many public lands and preserves, thanks to visionaries in the past who set the land aside. Amazingly, 26 species of orchids can still be found within Metropolitan Boston. Many of the towns along the north-south arc of Rt. 128 (it eventually becomes I-95 and then I-93) from its beginning at Gloucester on Cape Ann to its terminus at Braintree have public conservation lands—often with boardwalks in the swamps and bogs—where many orchid species can be found.

Blue Hills Reservation

At 7,000 acres, the massive Blue Hills Reservation—near the southern terminus of Rt. 128—provides a green oasis in the urban Boston environment. Twenty-two orchid species have been recorded in or adjacent to the Blue Hills over the years, and nearly all can still be found there. The season starts in middle-to late May with Pink Lady's-slippers and Large Whorled Pogonia and Arethusa can be found in some of the bogs by Memorial Day. Rose Pogonia and Tuberous Grass-Pink bloom in June, followed by various Twayblades, Rattlesnake Plantains and Purple Fringed Orchids. For more info:
http://www.mass.gov/dcr/parks/metroboston/blue.htm

Located at the other end of Rt. 128, the Cape Ann area offers many of the same spring-flowering species, blooming about a week later. The Manchester-Essex Conservation Trust manages several preserves in this area. For more info: http://00657f0.netsolhost.com/getoutdoors.html

Western Massachusetts: Mount Toby & The Notch

Mount Toby is a series of large hills located just east of the Connecticut River and north of Amherst. Extensive limestone deposits and diverse habitats are home to 34 species of orchids.

UMass Mt. Toby Forest Demonstration Forest

A 735-acre forest preserve used for teaching and research is open to the public and is a good place to search for orchids. Some areas are so inaccessible that they were never logged.
http://eco.umass.edu/facilities/our-forest-properties/mt-toby/

Greene Swamp Preserve

The centerpiece of this preserve is a 10-acre swamp; other features are a small stream and interesting rock outcrops on the southern slopes of Mt. Toby. Showy Lady's-slippers used to occur in Greene Swamp but have sadly been extirpated, due to over-collecting by the many colleges in the area. The preserve still supports a wide variety of orchid species.
http://www.nature.org/ourinitiatives/regions/northamerica/united-states/massachusetts/placesweprotect/greene-swamp-preserve.xml

The Notch

The Notch is located south of Amherst and is the highest point on Rt. 116 as it passes through the Holyoke Range. Although not as orchid-rich as Mt. Toby, 14 species have been found in the immediate vicinity of The Notch. The Notch Visitor Center, located at 1500 West St. in Amherst (413-253-2883) is open daily and is a good source for area info

CONNECTICUT
55 species and varieties

Northwest Highlands

Located in the northwestern corner of the state, this region contains some of Connecticut's last untouched natural areas. The unique geography of limestone forests, ridges and wetlands provide good orchid habitat.

Robbins Swamp

Located near Canaan, this 1,500 acre calcareous wetland is home to a significant population of Yellow Lady's-slippers.
http://www.nynjctbotany.org/lgtofc/robbinswp.html

RHODE ISLAND
39 species and varieties

Lime Rock Preserve

Located near Lincoln, this 137-acre Nature Conservancy preserve nurtures 30 species of rare plants, more than any other site in Rhode Island. The dolomitic marble found here produces a special calcareous soil that differs from the predominately acid soil of the rest of the state and provides a perfect habitat for Yellow Lady's-slipper and Northern Green Bog Orchid.
http://www.nature.org/ourinitiatives/regions/northamerica/united-states/rhodeisland/placesweprotect/lime-rock-preserve.xml

	MAY	JUNE	JULY	AUG	SEPT
Listera australis		pg. 84			
Galearis spectabilis		pg. 64			
Cypripedium arietinum		pg. 50			
Calypso bulbosa var. americana		pg. 36			
Cypripedium parviflorum		pg. 54			
Cypripedium acaule		pg. 48			
Coeloglossum viride var. virescens		pg. 38			
Isotria verticillata		pg. 76			
Corallorhiza trifida		pg. 45			
Aplectrum hyemale		pg. 30			
Arethusa bulbosa		pg. 32			
Platanthera hookeri		pg. 110			
Isotria medeoloides		pg. 74			
Spiranthes lucida		pg. 134			
Liparis liliifolia		pg. 78			
Pogonia ophioglossoides		pg. 126			
Liparis loeselii		pg. 80			
Platanthera dilatata var. dilatata		pg. 104			
Malaxis unifolia		pg. 92			
Cypripedium reginae		pg. 60			
Amerorchis rotundifolia		pg. 28			
Calopogon tuberosus var. tuberosus		pg. 34			
Platanthera obtusata subsp. obtusata			pg. 118		
Corallorhiza maculata var. maculata			pg. 40		
Platanthera huronensis			pg. 94		
Platanthera lacera			pg. 112		
Platanthera macrophylla			pg. 116		
Platanthera grandiflora			pg. 108		
Malaxis monophyllos var. brachypoda			pg. 90		
Platanthera blephariglottis			pg. 96		
Listera convallarioides			pg. 86		
Platanthera (Gymnadeniopsis) clavellata			pg. 100		
Epipactis helleborine			pg. 62		
Spiranthes lacera var. lacera			pg. 132		
Goodyera repens			pg. 70		
Goodyera pubescens			pg. 68		
Spiranthes romanzoffiana			pg. 138		
Platanthera psycodes			pg. 124		
Platanthera ciliaris			pg. 98		
Triphora trianthophora			pg. 146		
Tipularia discolor			pg. 144		
Spiranthes cernua					pg. 130
Corallorhiza odontorhiza var. odontorhiza					pg. 42
Spiranthes ochroleuca					pg. 136

BLOOM PHENOLOGY | **161**

References

This list includes many of the classic native orchid publications pertaining to the New England and New York region. Since 1995, two native orchid journals were born and include numerous interesting articles on New England and New York species: *North American Native Orchid Journal* and *The Native Orchid Conference Journal.* Space limitation prevents us from including most of the pertinent citations from these two journals.

Ackerman, J. D. 1975. Reproductive biology of *Goodyera oblongifolia* (Orchidaceae). Madrono 23: 191-198.

Ackerman, J. D. & M. R. Mesler. 1979. Pollination biology of *Listera cordata* (Orchidaceae). American Journal of Botany 66: 820-824.

Ames, O. 1906. *Habenaria orbiculata* and *Habenaria macrophylla.* Rhodora 8: 1-5.

Ames, O. 1909. Orchidaceae IV: The genus *Habenaria* in North America. Ames Botanical Laboratory, Boston.

Ames, O. 1921. Notes on New England orchids. 1. *Spiranthes.* Rhodora 23: 73-85.

Ames, O. 1922a. Notes on New England orchids. 2. The mycorrhia of *Goodyera pubescens.* Rhodora 24: 37-46.

Ames, O. 1922b. A discussion of *Pogonia* and its allies in the northeastern United States with reference to extra-limital genera and species. Orchidaceae 7: 3-38.

Ames, O. 1938. Resupination as a diagnostic character in the Orchidaceae with special reference to *Malaxis monophyllos.* Botanical Museum Leaflets, Harvard University 6: 145-183.

Andrews, A. L. 1901. A natural hybrid between *Habenaria lacera* and *H. psychodes.* Rhodora 3: 245-248.

Angelo, R. & D. E. Bufford. 2005. Atlas of the flora of New England: Orchidaceae. <http://neatlas.huh.harvard.edu>

Auclair, A. N. 1972. Comparative ecology of the orchids *Aplectrum hymale* and *Orchis spectabilis.* Bulletin of the Torrey Botanical Club 99: 1-10.

Baldwin, H. 1884. The orchids of New England. John Wiley & Sons, New York.

Baldwin, J. T. 1970. White phase in flower development in *Cypripedium acaule.* Rhodora 721: 142-143.

Bartlett, H. H. 1922. Color types of *Corallorhiza maculata* Raf. Rhodora 24: 145-158.

Bateman, R. M., K. E. James, Y.-B. Luo, R. K. Laure, T. Fulcher, P. J. Cribb, & M. Chase. 2009. Molecular phylogenetics and morphological reappraisal of the *Platanthera* clade (Orchidaceae: Orchidinae) prompts expansion of the generic limits of *Galearis* and *Platanthera.* Annals of Botany 104: 431-445.

Baxter, M. C. & H. D. House. 1925. The rare plants of Bergen Swamp. New York State Museum Bulletin 266: 103-106.

Bowles, M. L. 1983. The tallgrass prairie orchids *Platanthera leucophaea* (Nutt.) Lindl. and *Cypripedium candidum* Muhl. ex Wild.: some aspects of their status, biology, and ecology, and implications toward management. Natural Areas Journal 3: 14-37.

Boyden, T. C. 1982. The pollination biology of *Calypso bulbosa* var. *americana* (Orchidaceae): initial deception of bumblebee visitors. Oecologia 55: 178-184.

Brackley, F. E. 1979. *Cypripedium reginae* rediscovered in New Hampshire. Rhodora 81: 579-580.

Brackley, F. E. 1985. The orchids of New Hampshire. Rhodora 87: 1-117.

Brower, A.E. 1977. Ram's-head lady's-slipper (*Cypripedium arietinum* R. Br.) in Maine and its relevance to the Critical Areas Program. Planning Report 25. State Planning Office, Augusta, ME.

Brown, P. M. 1988. Stalking the wild orchids. Wild Flower Notes 3: 4-29.

Brown, P. M. 1992. *Platanthera pallida* (Orchidaceae), a new species of fringed orchis from Long Island, New York, USA. Novon 2: 308-311.

Brown, P. M. 1993. A field and study guide to the orchids of New England and New York. Orchis Press, Jamaica Plain, MA.

Brown, P. M. 1997a. Wild orchids of the northeastern United States. Cornell University Press, Ithaca.

Brown, P. M. 1997b. Taxonomy and distribution of *Spiranthes casei* Catling & Cruise in northern New England. Master's thesis. University of Massachusetts, Dartmouth.

Brown, P. M. 2002. Resurrection of the genus *Gymnadeniopsis* Rydb. North American Native Orchid Journal 8: 32-40.

Brown, P. M. 2007. Wild orchids of the Northeast. University Press of Florida, Gainesville.

Brown, P. M. 2008. *Platanthera pallida*, fifteen years of comparisons. North American Native Orchid Journal 14: 123-134.

Burrage, A. 1921. Notes on native New England orchids. Privately published.

Cameron, J. W. 1976. The orchids of Maine. University of Maine, Orono.

Cameron, K. M. 2005. Leave it to the leaves: a molecular phylogenetic study of Malaxideae (Epidendroideae: Orchidaceae). American Journal of Botany 92: 1025-1032.

Camp, W. H. 1940. A new variety of *Triphora*. Rhodora 42: 55-56.

Carpenter, G. M. 1959. A color variant of *Habenaria cristata*. Bulletin of the Torrey Botanical Club 86: 137-138.

Case, F. W. 1987. Orchids of the western Great Lakes region (revised edition). Cranbrook Institute of Science, Bulletin 48.

Catling, P. M. 1976. On the geographic distribution, ecology, and distinctive features of *Listera* ×*veltmanii* Case. Rhodora 78: 261-269.

Catling, P. M. 1978. Taxonomic notes on *Spiranthes casei* Catling & Cruise and *S.* × *intermedia* Ames. Rhodora 80: 377-389.

Catling, P. M. 1980a. Rain-assisted autogamy in *Liparis loeselii* (L.) L. C. Rich. (Orchidaceae). Bulletin of the Torrey Botanical Club 107: 525-529.

Catling, P. M. 1980b. Systematics of *Spiranthes* L. C. Richard in northeastern North America. Ph.D. thesis. University of Toronto.

Catling, P. M. 1981. Taxonomy of autumn-flowering *Spiranthes* species of southern Nova Scotia. Canadian Journal of Botany 59: 1253-1270.

Catling, P. M. 1982. Breeding systems of northeastern North American *Spiranthes* (Orchidaceae). Canadian Journal of Botany 60: 3017-3039.

Catling, P. M. 1983a. Autogamy in eastern Canadian Orchidaceae: a review of current knowledge and some new observations. Naturaliste Canadien 110: 37-53.

Catling, P. M. 1983b. Pollination of northeastern North American *Spiranthes* (Orchidaceae). Canadian Journal of Botany 61: 1080-1093.

Catling, P. M. 1991. Systematics of *Malaxis bayardii* and *M. unifolia*. Lindleyana 6: 3-23.

Catling, P. M. & V. Brownell. 1999a. *Platanthera lacera* ×*leucophaea*, a new cryptic natural hybrid, and a key to northeastern North American fringed-orchids. Canadian Journal of Botany 77: 1144-1149.

Catling, P. M., V. Brownell, & G. Allen. 1999b. A new natural hybrid fringed-orchid from Ontario. Lindleyana 14: 77-86.

Catling, P. M. & V. R. Catling. 1990. Anther cap retention in *Tipularia discolor*. Lindleyana 6: 113-116.

Catling, P. M. & V. R. Catling. 1991. A synopsis of breeding systems and pollination in North American orchids. Lindleyana 6: 187-210.

Catling, P. M. & V. R. Catling. 1994. Identification of *Platanthera lacera* hybrids (Orchidaceae) from New Brunswick and Nova Scotia. Lindleyana 9: 19-32.

Catling, P. M. & J. E. Cruise. 1974. *Spiranthes casei*, a new species from northeastern North America. Rhodora 76: 526-536.

Catling, P. M. & G. Knerer. 1980. Pollination of the small white lady's-slipper (*Cypripedium candidum*) in Lambton County, southern Ontario. Canadian Field Naturalist 94: 435-438.

Catling, P. M. & Z. Lucas. 1987. The status of *Calopogon tuberosus* var. *latifolius* with comments on the application of varietal rank. Rhodora 89: 401-413.

Catling, P. M. & C. J. Sheviak. 1993. Taxonomic notes on some North American orchids. Lindleyana 8: 80-81.

Chapman, W. K. 1997. Orchids of the Northeast. Syracuse University Press, Syracuse.

Child, H. W. 1922. A New England occurrence of *Listera australis*. Rhodora 24: 187-188.

Clute, W. N. 1898. *Pogonia verticillata* on Long Island. Plant World 1: 176.

Correll, D. S. 1941. A new *Spiranthes* hybrid from New Hampshire. American Orchid Society Bulletin 9: 241.

Correll, D. S. 1950. Native Orchids of North America. Chronica Botanica Co., Waltham, MA.

Darwin, C. 1862. On the various contrivances by which British and foreign orchids are fertilized by insects. J. Murray, London.

Davis, R. W. 1986. The pollination biology of *Cypripedium acaule* (Orchidaceae). Rhodora 88: 445-450.

Deane, W. 1891. The native orchids of New England. The American Gardener 12: 152-157.

Denslow, H. M. 1914. Notes on some orchids of Fairlee, Vt. Vermont Botanical Club Bulletin 9: 23-25.

Denslow, H. M. 1919. Reminiscences of orchid-hunting. Torreya 19: 152-156.

Denslow, H. M. 1920. Further reflections of an orchid hunter. Journal of The New York Botanical Garden 21: 145-156.

Denslow, H. M. 1924a. Native orchids of Manhattan Island. Journal of The New York Botanical Garden 25: 290-293.

Denslow, H. M. 1924b. *Isotria verticillata*. Addisonia 9: 33-34.

Denslow, H. M. 1927. Native orchids in and near New York. Torreya 27: 61-63.

Devos, N., O. Raspé, A.-L. Jacquemart, & D. Tyteca. 2006. On the monophyly of *Dactylorhiza* Necker ex Nevski (Orchidaceae): is *Coeloglossum viride* (L.) Hartman a *Dactylorhiza?* Botanical Journal of the Linnean Society 152: 261-269.

Drew, W. B. & R. A. Giles. 1951. *Epipactis helleborine* (L.) Cranz in Michigan, and its general range in North America. Rhodora 53: 240-242.

Dutton, D. L. 1927. *Listera australis* in Vermont. Vermont Botanical & Bird Clubs Joint Bulletin 12: 43-44.

Eastman, L. M. 1976. Nodding Pogonia. *Triphora trianthophora* (Sw.) Rydb., in Maine and its relevance to the Critical Areas Program. Planning Report No. 19. State Planning Office, Augusta, ME.

Eastman, L. M. 1988. *Calopogon tuberosus* var. *latifolius* (Saint-John) Boivin (Orchidaceae) new to the United States. Rhodora 90: 101.

Eastman, L. M., R. L. Hinkle, & D. M. Dumond. 1982. A new station for *Goodyera oblongifolia* Raf. in northern Maine. Rhodora 84: 311-313.

Effron, M. & E. C. Briggs. 1986. Rediscovery of *Isotria verticillata* (Willd.) Raf. (Orchidaceae) in Vermont. Rhodora 88: 47-48.

Fernald, M. L. 1899. The rattlesnake plantains of New England. Rhodora 1: 2-7.

Fernald, M. L. 1946. Some orchids of the Manual Range. Rhodora 48: 161-162.

Fernald, M. L. 1950. Gray's manual of botany, 8th ed. American Book Co., New York.

Flora of North America Editorial Committee, eds. 2002. Flora of North America, north of Mexico. Orchidaceae, Vol. 26: 490-651. Oxford University Press, New York.

Freudenstein, J. V. 1987. A preliminary study of *Corallorhiza maculata* (Orchidaceae) in eastern North America. Contributions from the University of Michigan Herbarium 16: 145-153.

Freudenstein, J. V. 1997. A monograph of *Corallorhiza* (Orchidaceae). Harvard Papers in Botany 1(10): 5-51.

Freudenstein, J. V. & D. M. Senyo. 2008. Relationships and evolution of *mat*K in a group of leafless orchids (*Corallorhiza* and Corallorhizinae: Orchidaceae: Epidendroideae). American Journal of Botany 95: 498-505.

Gleason, H. A. & A. Cronquist. 1991. Manual of vascular plants of northeastern United States and adjacent Canada, 2nd ed. The New York Botanical Garden, Bronx, NY.

Goldman, D. H., R. K. Jansen, C. van der Berg, I. J. Leitch, M. F. Fy, & M. W. Chase. 2004. Molecular and cytological examination of *Calopogon* (Orchidaceae: Epidendroideae): circumscription, phylogeny, polyploidy, and possible hybrid speciation. American Journal of Botany 91: 707-723.

Gray, A. 1862-1863. Fertilization of orchids. American Journal of Science 34: 420-429, 36: 292-294.

Gray, A. 1868. Monstrous flowers of *Habenaria fimbriata*. American Naturalist 2: 38.

Gray, A. 1879. *Epipactus helleborine*, var. *viridens* (*E. viridiflora*, Reichenbach), a North American plant. Botanical Gazette 4: 206.

Gustafso, N. A. H. 1933. A teratological specimen of *Cypripedium acaule* [from VT]. Rhodora 35: 263-264.

Haines, A. 2011. Flora Novae Angliae. Yale University Press, New Haven.

Haines, A. & T. F. Vining. 1998. Flora of Maine. V. F. Thomas Co., Bar Harbor.

Hogan, K. P. 1983. The pollination biology and breeding system of *Aplectrum hyemale* (Orchidaceae). Canadian Journal of Botany 61: 1906-1910.

Hollick, C. A. 1928. *Isotria verticillata* on Staten Island. Torreya 28: 75-77.

Homoya, M. A. 1977. Some aspects of the life history of *Isotria medeoloides*, an endangered orchid species. Transactions of the Illinois State Academy of Science 70: 196.

Homoya, M. A. 1993. Orchids of Indiana. Indiana Academy of Science, IN.

House, H. D. 1905. Further notes on the orchids of central New York. Bulletin of the Torrey Botanical Club 32: 373-382.

Hoy, J. M. 2001. *Listera auriculata* (Auricled Twayblade) conservation plan. New England Plant Conservation Program, Framingham, MA.

Hoy, J. M. 2002a. *Listera convallarioides* (Broad-leaved Twayblade) conservation and research plan for U.S. Forest Service Region 9. New England Wild Flower Society, Framingham, MA.

Hoy, J. M. 2002b. *Listera cordata* (Heart-Leaved Twayblade) conservation and research plan for U.S. Forest Service Region 9. New England Wild Flower Society, Framingham, MA.

Jones, L. R. 1902. *Pogonia affinis* in Vermont. Rhodora 4: 216-217.

Kalbfleisch, A. S. 1898. Orchids on Long Island. Plant World 1: 177-179.

Kallunki, J. A. 1976. Population studies in *Goodyera* (Orchidaceae) with emphasis on the hybrid origin of *G. tesselata*. Brittonia 28: 53-75.

Kallunki, J. A. 1981. Reproductive biology of mixed-species populations of *Goodyera* (Orchidaceae) in northern Michigan. Brittonia 33: 137-155.

Keenan, P. E. 1983. A complete guide to Maine's orchids. DeLorme, Freeport.

Keenan, P. E. 1986a. New stations for *Platanthera flava* and *Triphora trianthophora* and other observations. Rhodora 88: 409-412.

Keenan, P. E. 1986b. Wild orchids in New England. American Orchid Society Bulletin 55: 696-699.

Keenan, P. E. 1987. The bloom sequence of wild orchids in New England. American Orchid Society Bulletin 56: 1059-1061.

Keenan, P. E. 1988a. *Calypso bulbosa*: hider of the north. American Orchid Society Bulletin 57: 375-377.

Keenan, P. E. 1988b. Progress report on *Isotria medeoloides*. American Orchid Society Bulletin 57: 624-626.

Keenan, P. E. 1989a. The wonderful world of *Cypripedium*. American Orchid Society Bulletin 58: 450-455.

Keenan, P. E. 1989b. Butterflies of the orchid world. American Orchid Society Bulletin 58: 767-771.

Keenan, P. E. 1990a. Documentation of the longevity of *Goodyera pubescens* leaves and update on *Triphora trianthophora* in New Hampshire. Rhodora 92: 126-128.

Kennan, P. E. 1990b. The big little green orchids. American Orchid Society Bulletin 59: 228-233.

Keenan, P. E. 1990c. The pigtails of the orchid world. American Orchid Society Bulletin 59: 683-687.

Keenan, P. E. 1991a. The mighty pogonias. American Orchid Society Bulletin 60: 338-341.

Keenan, P. E. 1991b. The American orchises. American Orchid Society Bulletin 60: 536-538.

Keenan, P. E. 1992a. A new form of *Triphora trianthophora* (Swartz) Rydberg, and part three of observations on the ecology of *Triphora trianthophora* (Orchidaceae) in New Hampshire. Rhodora 94: 38-42.

Keenan, P. E. 1992b. Grass-pinks. American Orchid Society Bulletin 61: 343-347.

Keenan, P. E. 1993. Thoreau's orchids. American Orchid Society Bulletin 62: 363-371.

Keenan, P. E. 1994a. Pretty in pink. American Orchid Society Bulletin 63: 250-255.

Keenan, P. E. 1994b. The coral-roots. American Orchid Society Bulletin 63: 512-517.

Keenan, P. E. 1995. Diversity in *Cypripedium acaule*. North American Native Orchid Journal 1: 201-210.

Keenan, P. E. 1996. Further observations on *Triphora trianthophora*: part 4. North American Native Orchid Journal 2: 196-209.

Keenan, P. E. 1999. Wild orchids across North America: a botanical travelogue. Timber Press, Portland.

Keenan, P. E. 2000. A short history of the genus *Cypripedium*. North American Native Orchid Journal 5: 29-42.

Klier, K., M. J. Leoschke, & J. F. Wendel. 1991. Hybridization and introgression in white and yellow lady's-slipper orchids (*Cypripedium candidum* and *C. pubescens*). Journal of Heredity 82: 305-318.

Lamont, E. E. 1992. East Hampton orchids: will they survive? Long Island Botanical Society Newsletter 2: 4-5.

Lamont, E. E. 1994. The weed orchid (*Epipactis helleborine*) on Long Island, New York. Long Island Botanical Society Newsletter 4: 12.

Lamont, E. E. 1995. Fanny Mulford's orchid collections from the late 1890s. Long Island Botanical Society Newsletter 5: 7-9.

Lamont, E. E. 1996a. Atlas of the orchids of Long Island, New York. Bulletin of the Torrey Botanical Club 123: 157-166.

Lamont, E. E. 1996b. One hundred years of change in the orchid flora of Long Island, New York. Program and Abstracts, Proceedings of the New York Natural History Conference 4: 20.

Lamont, E. E. 1998. Notes on wild orchids of Long Island, New York. Long Island Botanical Society Newsletter 8: 36.

Lamont, E. E. 2000. Historical orchid collections from Brooklyn, New York. North American Native Orchid Journal 6: 93-102.

Lamont, E. E. 2001a. Notes on the white-fringed orchid on Long Island, New York. Long Island Botanical Society Newsletter 11: 46.

Lamont, E. E. 2001b. An additional note on the white-fringed orchid on Long Island, New York. Long Island Botanical Society Newsletter 11: 47.

Lamont, E. E. 2007. One hundred fifty years of change in the orchid flora of Brooklyn and Queens, New York. Transactions of the Linnaean Society of New York 10: 123-132.

Lamont, E. E., J. M. Beitel, & R. E. Zaremba. 1988. Current status of orchids on Long Island, New York. Bulletin of the Torrey Botanical Club 115: 113-121.

Latham, R. 1927. *Tipularia uniflora* on Montauk Point, Long Island. Torreya 27: 51.

Latham, R. 1940. Distribution of wild orchids on Long Island. Long Island Forum 3: 103-107.

Latham, R. 1971. The crane-fly orchid on Long Island. Engelhartia 4: 55.

Lowenstein, A. E. 1917. Orchids found in the region of Asquam Lake [NH]. Rhodora 19: 56-57.

Luer, C. A. 1972. The native orchids of Florida. The New York Botanical Garden, Bronx.

Luer, C. A. 1975. The native orchids of the United States and Canada, excluding Florida. The New York Botanical Garden, Bronx.

Magee, D. W. & H. A. Ahles. 1999. Flora of the northeast: a manual of the vascular flora of New England and adjacent New York. University of Massachusetts Press, Amherst.

McGrath, R. T. 2008. Contributions to the status and morphology of *Platanthera pallida*, Pale Fringed Orchis. Long Island Botanical Society Newsletter 18: 1-6.

McGrath, R. T. & J. L. Turner. 1985. Some orchids of the Long Island pine barrens. The Heath Hen 2: 32-39.

Mehrhoff, L. A. 1980. Reproductive systems in the genus *Isotria* (Orchidaceae). Botanical Society of America, Misc. Ser. Pub. 158: 72.

Mehrhoff, L. A. 1983. Pollination in the genus *Isotria* (Orchidaceae). American Journal of Botany 70: 1444-1453.

Millspaugh, C. F. 1884. The Droseraceae and Orchidaceae of Spruce Pond, N.Y. Bulletin of the Torrey Botanical Club 11: 271-272.

Mitchell, R. S. & G. C. Tucker. 1997. Revised checklist of New York State plants. New York State Museum Bulletin 490, Albany.

Morris, F. & E. A. Eames. 1929. Our wild orchids. Charles Scribner's Sons, New York.

Mosquin, T. 1970. The reproductive biology of *Calypso bulbosa* (Orchidaceae). Canadian Field-Naturalist 84: 291-296.

Mously, H. 1925. Further notes on *Calypso*. Journal of the New York Botanical Garden 25: 25-32.

Muenscher, W. C. 1946. The vegetation of Bergen Swamp. I. The vascular plants. Proceedings of the Rochester Academy of Sciences 9: 64-117.

Native Orchid Conservation. 2005. Orchids of Manitoba. Native Orchid Conservation, Inc., Winnipeg.

Nelson, T. 2009. Searching for Long Island's wild orchids. Long Island Botanical Society Newsletter 19: 1-6.

Nelson, T. 2010. A great orchid hunting year: tales from the field in 2009. Native Orchid Conference Journal 7: 16-20.

Niles, G. G. 1904. Bog trotting for orchids. Knickerbocker Press, New York.

Nylander, O. O. 1922. Life history of Calypso. Maine Naturalist 2: 82-83.

Nylander, O. O. 1935. Our northern orchids. Star-Herald Publ. Co., Presque Isle, ME.

Platt, J. L., E. Yanuck-Platt, & C. J. Sheviak. 1986. A new station for *Listera auriculata* (Orchidaceae) in New York State. Rhodora 84: 547-549.

Ramsey, C. T. 1950. The triggered rostellum of the genus *Listera*. American Orchid Society Bulletin 19: 482-485.

Ramsey, C. T. 1966. Our two purple-fringed orchids. American Orchid Society Bulletin 35: 458-460.

Raup, H. M. 1930. The pollination of *Habenaria obtusata*. Rhodora 32: 88-89.

Reddoch, A. H. & J. M. Reddoch. 1993. The species pair *Platanthera orbiculata* and *P. macrophylla* (Orchidaceae): taxonomy, morphology, distributions and habits. Lindleyana 8: 171-187.

Richburg, J. A. 2003. *Aplectrum hyemale* (Muhl. ex Willd.) Nutt., Puttyroot. Conservation and research plan for New England. New England Wild Flower Society, Framingham, MA.

Risen, K. & C. Risen. 2010. Orchids of the North Woods. Kollath+Stensaas Publishing, Duluth, MN.

Rooney, B. M. 1917. Orchids of St. Johnsbury. Vermont Botanical & Bird Clubs Joint Bulletin 2: 29.

Seymour, F. C. 1982. The flora of New England, 2nd ed. Phytologia Memoirs 5. Plainfield, NJ.

Sheviak, C. J. 1974. An introduction to the ecology of the Illinois Orchidaceae. Illinois State Museum Scientific Papers XIV, Springfield.

Sheviak, C. J. 1982. Biosystematic study of the *Spiranthes cernua* complex. New York State Museum Bulletin 448, Albany.

Sheviak, C. J. 1990. Biological considerations in the management of temperate terrestrial orchid habitats. In: R. S. Mitchell, C. J. Sheviak, & D. J. Leopold, eds., Ecosystem management: rare species and significant habitats. New York State Museum Bulletin 471: 194-196.

Sheviak, C. J. 1991. Morphological variation in the compilospecies *Spiranthes cernua* (L.) L. C. Rich.: ecologically limited effects of gene flow. Lindleyana 6: 228-234.

Sheviak, C. J. 1993. *Cypripedium parviflorum* Salisb. var. *makasin* (Farwell) Sheviak. American Orchid Society Bulletin 62: 403.

Sheviak, C. J. 1994a. *Cypripedium parviflorum* Salisb. I: the small-flowered varieties. American Orchid Society Bulletin 63: 664-669.

Sheviak, C. J. 1994b. A new look at the taxonomy of our yellow lady's-slippers. New York Flora Association Newsletter 5: 3-4.

Sheviak, C. J. 1995. *Cypripedium parviflorum* Salisbury part 2: the larger flowered plants and patterns of variation. American Orchid Society Bulletin 64: 606-612.

Sheviak, C. J. 1999. The identies of *Platanthera hyperborea* and *P. huronensis*, with the description of a new species from North America. Lindleyana 14: 193-203.

Sheviak, C. J. 2001. A role for water droplets in the pollination of *Platanthera aquilonis* (Orchidaceae). Rhodora 103: 380-386.

Sheviak, C. J. 2011. *Cypripedium montanum* in the east? Native Orchid Conference Journal 8(4): 7-22.

Sheviak, C. J. 2011. *Platanthera huronensis* in the north, and the occurrence of *P. hyperborea* in North America. Native Orchid Conference Journal 8(2): 14-36.

Sheviak, C. J. and M. L. Bowles. 1986. The prairie fringed orchids: a pollinator-isolated pair. Rhodora 88: 267-290.

Sheviak, C. J. & P. M. Catling. 1980. The identity and status of *Spiranthes ochroleuca* (Rydberg) Rydberg. Rhodora 82: 525-562.

Smith, G. R. & G. E. Snow. 1976. Pollination ecology of *Platanthera* (*Habenaria*) *ciliaris* and *P. blephariglottis* (Orchidaceae). Botanical Gazette 137: 133-140.

St.Hilaire, L. 2002. *Amerorchis rotundifolia*: Conservation and research plan for New England. New England Wildflower Society, Framingham, MA.

Stoutamire, W. P. 1967. Flower biology of the lady's-slippers (Orchidaceae, *Cypripedium*). Michigan Botanist 6: 159-173.

Stoutamire, W. P. 1968. Mosquito pollination of *Habenaria obtusata* (Orchidaceae). Michigan Botanist 7: 203-212.

Stoutamire, W. P. 1971. Pollination in temperate American orchids. Pages 233-243. In: M. J. G. Corrigan et al., eds., Proceedings of the 6th World Orchid Conference. Halstead Press, Sydney, Australia.

Stoutamire, W. P. 1974. Relationships of the purple-fringed orchids *Platanthera psycodes* and *P. grandiflora*. Brittonia 26: 42-58.

Stoutamire, W. P. 1978. Pollination of *Tipularia discolor*, an orchid with modified symmetry. American Orchid Society Bulletin 47: 413-415.

Thein, L. B. 1969. Mosquito pollination of *Habenaria obtusata* (Orchidaceae). American Journal of Botany 56: 232-237.

Thien, L. B. & B. G. Marcks. 1972. The floral biology of *Arethusa bulbosa*, *Calopogon tubersosus* and *Pogonia ophioglossoides* (Orchidaceae). Canadian Journal of Botany 50: 2319-2325.

Torrey, R. 1924. Wild orchids at Montauk. New York Evening Post [July 14].

Upham, A. U. 1942. *Epipactis latifolia* in New Hampshire. Rhodora 44: 456-457.

Voss, E. G. & R. E. Riefner. 1983. A pyralid moth (Lepidoptera) as pollinator of blunt-leaf orchid. Great Lakes Entomologist 16: 57-60.

Wallace, J. E. 1951. The orchids of Maine. University of Maine Bulletin 53: 1-80.

Wallace, L. E. 2002. An evaluation of taxonomic boundaries in *Platanthera dilatata* (Orchidaceae). Rhodora 105: 322-336.

Wallace, L. E. 2003. Molecular evidence for allopolyploid speciation and recurrent origins in *Platanthera huronensis* (Orchidaceae). International Journal of Plant Sciences 164: 907-916.

Wallace, L. E. 2004. A comparison of genetic variation & structure in the allopolyploid *Platanthera huronensis* and its diploid progenitors, *Platanthera aquilonis* and *Platanthera dilatata* (Orchidaceae). Canadian Journal of Botany 82: 244-252.

Wallace, L. E. 2006. Spatial genetic structure and frequency of interspecific hybridization in *Platanthera aquilonis* and *P. dilatata* (Orchidaceae) occurring in sympatry. American Journal of Botany 93: 1001-1009.

Wallace, L. E. & M. A. Case. 2000. Contrasting allozyme diversity between northern and southern populations of *Cypripedium parviflorum* (Orchidaceae): implications for Pleistocene refugia and taxonomic boundaries. Systematic Botany 25: 281-296.

Weatherby, C. A. 1920. *Habenaria psycodes* var. *ecalcarta* in Vermont. Rhodora 22: 31-32.

Weldy, T. & D. Werier. 2012. New York flora atlas. New York Flora Association, Albany. <http://atlas.nyfa.org>

Whighman, D. F. & M. McWethy. 1980. Studies on the pollination ecology of *Tipularia discolor* (Orchidaceae). American Journal of Botany 67: 550-555.

Williams, S. A. 1994. Observations on reproduction in *Triphora trianthophora* (Orchidaceae). Rhodora 96: 30-43.

Zenkert, C. A. 1930. *Serapias helleborine* in Buffalo and vicinity. Torreya 20: 46-50.

Zenkert, C. A. 1950. The story of an immigrant orchid. American Orchid Society Bulletin 19: 316-318.

Zika, P. F. 1983. *Triphora trianthophora* in Massachusetts and Vermont. Rhodora 85: 123-124.

Index

Quick Orchid Finder

Other user-friendly guides from Kollath-Stensaas

Lichens of the North Woods

Insects of New England & New York

Moths & Caterpillars of the North Woods

Spiders of the North Woods

Fascinating Fungi of New England

Earthworms of the Great Lakes

Learn more about our books and authors at
www.kollathstensaas.com